FORGIVENESS
MAKES YOU
FREE

"*Forgiveness Makes You Free* is a gift of mercy from the hand of God. It tells the story of a priest who learned, step by step, to follow after Jesus and to present himself as a 'living offering' to God, who learned how to pray, how to forgive, how to resist the enemy, and how to receive the gifts God wanted to give him. Above all, it shows how he learned to follow after Jesus, no matter how much it cost him."

From the foreword by **Immaculée Ilibagiza**
Author of *Left to Tell*

"Fr. Ubald lives and proclaims a message of freedom and healing that is greatly needed in the Church today. The whole world has heard of the genocide in Rwanda; now it is time for the world to hear the story of redemption happening there. This is a hopeful and inspiring message."

Neal Lozano
Founder of Heart of the Father Ministries
and author of *Unbound*

"'In the name of Jesus, I forgive you.' Fr. Ubald's emotional and courageous story of forgiveness spoke to my heart. His painful yet joyful journey of mercy has borne fruit, annunciating how the healing power of forgiveness can set you free and turn enemies into brothers and sisters in Christ."

Christina Lynch
Director of psychological services
St. John Vianney Theological Seminary

"In our work with Renewal Ministries, we have known and worked with Fr. Ubald Rugirangoga since 2005. In that time, we have seen how the five keys explored in *Forgiveness Makes You Free* have healed and set thousands free."

Lloyd and Nancy Greenhaw
Country coordinators for Renewal Ministries

"With each turn of the page, I yearned evermore to experience the peace Fr. Ubald Rugirangoga preached—a peace that comes from forgiving what seems humanly impossible to forgive; a peace that comes when we release the wounds of the past, especially the wounds that were inflicted by those closest to us; a peace that surpasses all understanding. Through powerful and poignant stories, Fr. Ubald allowed me to step into his shoes and showed me how to walk in forgiveness and mercy, two actions that bring freedom and healing and result in peace and joy. If you have ever had your faith shaken by suffering, struggled with forgiveness, or longed for the peace of Christ to rule your heart, this book is for you!"

Kelly M. Wahlquist
Founder of WINE: Women In the New Evangelization

"This dramatic and heart-wrenching personal retelling of the Rwandan genocide in 1994 calls all of its readers to spiritual healing. Only in a personal relationship with Jesus Christ can true freedom in lasting peace be found. In *Forgiveness Makes You Free*, Fr. Ubald Rugirangoga shares many stories of people from all over the world, including Europe and America, who came to true forgiveness and offered it to others."

Most Rev. David L. Ricken
Bishop of Green Bay

"*Forgiveness Makes You Free* is a poignant testament to the experience and power of forgiveness even in the face of horrific events. Fr. Ubald's reflections on forgiveness, mercy, and reconciliation highlight both their distinctive features and their interrelationship in the context of peace and justice."

Laura Miller-Graff
Assistant Professor of Psychology and Peace Studies
University of Notre Dame

FORGIVENESS
MAKES YOU
FREE

A Dramatic Story of Healing
and Reconciliation from the
Heart of Rwanda

FR. UBALD RUGIRANGOGA

WITH HEIDI HESS SAXTON

FOREWORD BY IMMACULÉE ILIBAGIZA

AVE MARIA PRESS AVE Notre Dame, Indiana

Interior photograph on page 98 © 2018 by KG Fine Photos.

Interior photographs on pages xvii, xviii, xxii, 22, 25, 36, 45, 49, 56, 62, 66, 74, 75, 82, 121, and 123 © 2018 by Katsey Long.

Interior photographs on pages xxiii, xxiv, xxv, 3, 4, 30, 44, 124, and 132 © 2018 by Craig R. Saxton.

Foreword © 2018 by Immaculée Ilibagiza

Founded in 1865, Ave Maria Press is a ministry of the United States Province of Holy Cross.

www.avemariapress.com

Paperback: ISBN-13 978-1-59471-871-7

E-book: ISBN-13 978-1-59471-872-4

Cover design by Kristen Hornyak Bonelli and Katherine Robinson.

Text design by Katherine Robinson.

Map illustration by Kristen Hornyak Bonelli.

Printed and bound in Canada.

Library of Congress Cataloging-in-Publication Data is available.

CONTENTS

⊷⊱✕⊰⊶

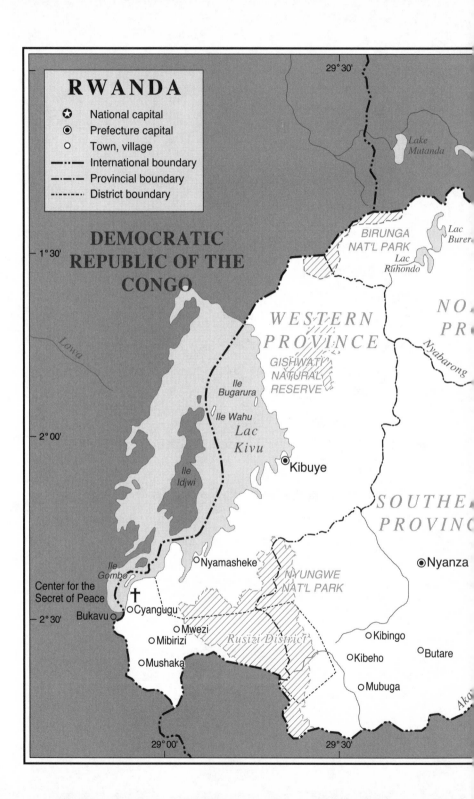

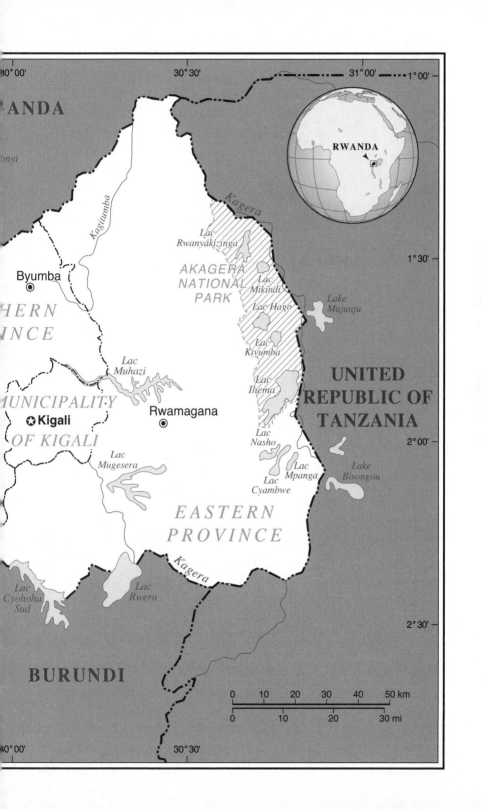

FOREWORD

✠

I was so happy when Fr. Ubald agreed to meet with me, face-to-face, at the Christus Center in Kigali, Rwanda, in the fall of 2000. "What can I do for you?" he asked. Though I was quite in awe of him, his kind eyes and gentle tone put me at ease right away. Like me, he had survived the Rwandan genocide. But while I had moved to the United States to start a new life, he had remained in Rwanda, preaching and using his gifts of healing to help those who had been so deeply wounded. God has used him over and over again to help bring people who were once mortal enemies back together as brothers and sisters in Christ, and I am so grateful to now be able to introduce this kind and loving priest to my new country.

It was 1992, and I was a college student the first time I heard Fr. Ubald preach at a healing service on my college campus. I had heard of a priest who preached forgiveness and healed people, and I wanted to find out more. I watched, fascinated, as with great boldness he led the people to seek deliverance and healing. "Go out! Go out!" he would shout at the spirits. Then, to the people, "The evil one has no place here! Pray with me! Hail, Mary . . ." And the people would raise their voices and cry out, calling to heaven as a mighty army of faith. "Our Father, who art in heaven . . ." The room rang with victory. Yes, even before the genocide, Jesus was touching people's lives through Fr. Ubald, reminding us of God's living presence among us. I saw many, many people delivered.

It was around this same time that I also heard of the messages of Our Lady of Kibeho, which was approved by the Vatican in 1991. Over and over, the Blessed Mother told those who would listen that souls need prayer like flowers need water; without prayer, our souls wither and are easily ensnared by evil. At that time, God was pouring out his Spirit on his people, trying to draw them close to him to avert the tragic violence that would soon erupt. And some people did pray—but not enough.

Each time I saw Fr. Ubald process through the crowd, blessing people with Jesus in the Eucharist, I saw people respond. After each procession, Father would proclaim what Jesus had done that day. "Someone is supposed to have an operation. Jesus wants you to know you don't need it anymore. Go to your doctor and have him examine you," Father would say. Then another, and another: a woman healed of infertility, someone's ear sore or leg wound healed, or a mental illness released.

"Go home and see your doctor, and get confirmation," he would say. "Then come back and give testimony, and thank God for what he has done for you." And people did. Time after time, people would stand and give witness of having been to a prayer service and claimed their healing— and had it confirmed by their own doctor. This happened first in Rwanda and later in the United States and Europe. You will meet some of these people in this book.

FR. UBALD COMES TO THE UNITED STATES

When I first reached the United States and began telling my story, many people came to me and told me how much my story had blessed them, how God had used my story to show them why they needed to forgive too. I would think to myself, "Oh, if they could only meet Fr. Ubald. Then they would really experience something powerful!"

And so, in 2009 I invited Father to come with me to one of my talks, and I saw people respond to him just as they had in Rwanda. The Holy Spirit used Fr. Ubald in a powerful way to bring a message of forgiveness and healing to those who most needed to hear it.

I am so grateful to be able to introduce this wonderful priest to my new homeland and allow people here to experience this encounter with Jesus through five spiritual keys of faith: seeing God at work, forgiving, resisting evil, choosing to live for Christ, and receiving God's blessing. When I was young, I remember hearing my mother coughing and coughing because she had asthma. Her illness affected all of us who loved her. And the same is true when someone has cancer or another illness: their sickness causes many people to suffer. The opposite is also true: when one person is healed, the whole family is healed.

In this country, people opened their hearts to me because of my story. They have listened to my story and received the truth of it in a way that often people in my own country cannot understand. Jesus said, "A prophet is not without honor except in his native place and among his own kin and in his own house" (Mk 6:4). In many ways, Fr. Ubald's message—both in his preaching and in this book— will bear much fruit in the lives of people outside Rwanda because of this. Each time he proclaims the power of God to release us from the wounds of the past, he gives people hope to come to Jesus for healing too.

THE RWANDAN GENOCIDE: TWENTY-FIVE YEARS LATER

It is a work of grace that this book is coming out on the twenty-fifth anniversary of the Rwandan genocide. How I wish there were many more like it! Although Rwanda has come very far in healing the divisions among people, we still have far to go. We are still healing. And the more light that is shed on those wounds, the more we are challenged to look not at what we lost but at the lessons we have learned that can become gifts for the world. Oh, how the world needs to learn from what we have suffered!

Sadly, there are still many people in Rwanda who are unable to hear the message of forgiveness because they are too caught up in their own pain and loss. Even my own brother, who was not living in Rwanda at the time of the genocide, struggled for years to listen to my story of how God helped me forgive the people who had murdered those

I love so much. Over and over I asked God to show me how to help him, but each time I tried, my brother would turn away from me, too upset to listen.

It wasn't until I wrote my book that he finally began to work through his feelings. He slowly read my story and realized not just what I had gone through but also how God's hand had been upon me so that I would live to tell not only of the evil I had experienced but also of the grace I had found.

In Rwanda it is difficult for me to tell my story the way I do in the United States. In Rwanda, if you speak of tribes— Hutu and Tutsi—people resist. For many people, this is no longer something to be discussed, no longer an important part of a person's identity. And yet, when I speak in America of the ethnic divisions that are part of my country's history, people listen. They understand what it means to be divided from others or to be treated differently because of an accident of birth—of race or ethnicity. They listen to my story, and of the divisions between Hutu and Tutsi, and think of the violence that has been part of their own story, where the words "black" and "white" have so much historic and cultural weight. When they hear where it all ended—of the hatred, the violence, and the victimization of those who are different—they say, "Thank you for helping me. Thank you for telling your story. It has helped me see my brother as another person. It has helped me to see how much I still need to forgive."

Here in the United States, Fr. Ubald's story of division will have great impact. It is not racial—and yet the outcome of the discrimination is there. Every evil manifests itself in the same way, whether as the Tutsi or Hutu, or as white, black, or brown. Our stories from Rwanda have helped people in the United States understand where we have been and where we are going unless we change. If you are at all interested in going through a healing process, you must do it. There is nothing good about these divisions; they only cause bad and evil. And yet, it is not too late to receive God's grace. "If then my people, upon whom my name has been pronounced, humble themselves and pray, and seek my face and turn from their evil ways, I will hear them from heaven and pardon their sins and heal their land" (2 Chr 7:14).

It will take time, but it can happen. Not long ago I returned to my village and met a man who had participated in the killings. He said to me, "You really want to know how I feel? I miss the people I killed."

I was shocked. What did he mean?

"Look at what we did to ourselves," he continued. "Look at the road—it is growing grass because no one is passing by. The things we took, they were gone in a month— but these people, our neighbors, they are gone forever. We thought that, by killing them, our enemies would be defeated. Instead, they just rose up from within our own tribe.

"I know you are a preacher," he said to me. "I am not. But I have seen these things. And I know that this was wrong. It was like a hurricane going through my mind, telling me that it will always be this way. But after the hurricane, the truth emerged. I knew, and could not avoid, the truth of what I had done."

I prayed with this man for peace. All the emotions that he had pushed down for so long had risen to the top, like cream. All the strong emotions, at some point in your life, will rise to the top and remind you, accuse you of what you have done. These things must be faced and dealt with. It may happen on your deathbed, but it must come out.

Listen to Our Lady of Kibeho

When Our Lady appeared to the schoolgirls at Kibeho in 1981, her message was for the whole world—not just for Rwanda. She showed the children the pain that was coming to our country, saying, "If you will listen to me, it will not come. If you do not listen, it will come not only to Rwanda but to the whole world." I have spoken and written about her message, which the whole world still needs to hear: love one another, forgive one another, and pray with one another. Help one another. It's all about love.

Forgiveness Makes You Free is a gift of mercy from the hand of God. It tells the story of a priest who grappled with his own vocation, his own weaknesses, and his own losses and grief. It tells the story of a man who learned, step by step, to follow Jesus and to present himself as a "living sacrifice" to God (see Romans 12:1). It shows how God brought people into Fr. Ubald's life who taught him how to pray, how to forgive, how to resist the enemy, and how to receive the gifts God wanted to give him. Above all, it shows how he learned to follow Jesus, no matter how much it cost him.

Fr. Ubald's message of showing mercy as a pathway to experiencing true forgiveness and encountering the healing touch of Christ is much needed today. Our Lady reminds us that even the most pious person can become lukewarm and be overcome by evil unless they continue to pray. "Let the leaders of the churches teach love and forgiveness, remind people to love and accept one another as creatures of God. Lay people, pick up your rosaries and pray from your heart." We did not listen, and the violence swept across our land. Will you listen? Will you pray, and will you forgive? What happened in Rwanda can happen anywhere.

But by the mercy of God, through the intercession of Our Lady, there is still time to turn the tide. Forgiveness makes you free. Are you ready to experience that freedom and to work so that others might receive the reconciliation and healing they so desperately need?

Our Lady of Kibeho, pray for us!

God bless you,
Immaculée Ilibagiza
June 6, 2018

PROLOGUE

My name is Fr. Ubald Rugirangoga. I was born the eldest
son of James Kabera and Anysie Mukaruhamya, devout
Christian parents of Tutsi ethnicity. Our village was in the
Nyamasheke district of Rwanda.

As a priest, I have often celebrated with my people the
Sacrament of Reconciliation, listening to confessions and
giving absolution to the souls seeking peace and pardon.
This forgiveness comes at great cost; it was necessary for
Jesus to lay down his life to atone for sin and restore us into
relationship with the Father. And yet, he gives these healing
graces to us freely, as a precious gift of mercy.

Fr. Ubald Rugirangoga

As a survivor of the Rwandan genocide against the Tutsi people, I have also witnessed the power of forgiveness to heal and restore beyond the confessional. In my own country and in foreign lands, I have witnessed countless thousands of people who, having encountered Jesus in the Eucharist, have laid down their burdens of hate and revenge, and opened their hearts to receive healing and peace. These men and women have discovered, just as I have, that forgiveness makes us free. It heals us. I have seen it. And I have lived it.

"FATHER, I MUST BEG PARDON. I KILLED YOUR MOTHER."

In 2005, I met Straton Sinzabakwira, who was burgomaster of the Karengera Commune where my family fled for safety during the genocide, as former friends and neighbors banded together to take nearly a million Tutsi lives, as well as the lives of Hutus who refused to join in the genocide. The genocide was ruthlessly organized and carried out with a single goal in mind: to wipe from the earth any trace of Tutsi ethnicity. In those days, blood flowed like water in Rwanda, the land of a thousand hills. And this man gave the order that took the lives of eighty-five members of my own family.

Fr. Ubald with Straton Sinzabakwira (right)

The genocide against the Tutsi people, which began on April 6, 1994, with the death of Rwandan president Juvénal Habyarimana, was finally halted by the Tutsi-dominated Rwandan Patriotic Front (RPF) in early July of the same year. At that time, the Hutu government in Kigali was overthrown, and those Hutus responsible for the killings feared being called to justice. Along with hundreds of thousands of Hutus, Straton and his family fled to the Congo. When war erupted there two years later, many political refugees were forced to return to Rwanda.[1]

While some of those who had been in positions of leadership and influence under the previous government were given help to escape to other countries, Straton was among the first to return voluntarily to Rwanda in order to take responsibility and tell the truth about what had happened. He was immediately recognized as one of the organizers of the genocide and was sent to prison. During the twenty-two years he spent in prison, he narrowly escaped death three times at the hands of those who did not want the truth to come to light.

In 1998, Straton first heard me preach about forgiveness as the only way to peace. When he heard my story, he recognized that it had been my family who had come to him for sanctuary and knew that one day he would have to beg my pardon. "It was the militia who killed them, but I gave the order," he said.

In 2005, Straton was called to give witness at the Gacaca courts, the ritual courts of justice where the truth was laid bare before those who had suffered the violence as well as those who had committed it. As about one hundred people gathered on the soft grass on the grounds of Nyamasheke district, victims and perpetrators together, to establish the truth of what had happened, Straton rose and announced that before he would testify, he needed to beg pardon . . . to me. It was then that I officially learned for the first time that my mother and my entire family had been killed at the Karengera Commune on April 17, 1994.

Straton's words cut me more deeply than any sword. How could I possibly show mercy toward the man who had destroyed all who were most dear to me in this world? And yet, if I did not forgive, how could I continue the work of reconciliation I believed God had called me to do?

God, help me. Help me to show mercy, I prayed as I approached the man where he stood and faced him. And then I felt my arms reaching out to hug him, and out of my own mouth came a miracle: "In the name of Jesus, I forgive you." His eyes widened, and as he shook my hand with both of his, I wondered what I must do for that forgiveness to bear the fruit of mercy.

God worked a great miracle that day. He put mercy into my heart for this man and his family. And out of my pain, and the pain of so many others, he has created something beautiful. It is called the Center for the Secret of Peace.

INTRODUCTION

*About Fr. Ubald Rugirangoga
and the Center for the Secret of Peace*

Imana yirirwa ahandi igataha mu Rwanda.
God spends the day elsewhere but sleeps in
Rwanda.

—Rwandan proverb

Soaring above Lake Kivu is the Center for the Secret of
Peace, a seventy-five-acre retreat center near the city of
Rusizi on the southeast shore in Rwanda. Walking near the
lake, pilgrims catch a glimpse of Our Lady of Kibeho, protected in an open-air shrine, before they ascend the stairway
and kneel before a second shrine, dedicated to Divine Mercy.
At the top of the hill near the space where they gather for
Mass is a third shrine dedicated to Our Lady of Love, for
without love there is no peace. Many infertile women have
been healed through her intercession. She offers benediction
to her children, waiting patiently for them to come home
to her. And so they do, though many of them do not know
exactly what they need. And yet it is so often here that they
find it.

Blessed by the bishop of the Cyangugu diocese of
Rwanda in 2016, the center draws thousands of pilgrims
who come in search of the peace that has eluded them. They
make the Stations of the Cross, pray the Divine Rosary chap-
let, and wait excitedly for the healing service to begin. On
the thirteenth of each month is a special service commemorating the anniversary of the apparitions of Fatima. It is not

uncommon for ten to thirty thousand people to gather for one of these Masses—even in the middle of the week.

Despite all they have endured, the people of Rwanda are a people of deep and abiding faith. Of the six hundred thousand Christians in the Cyangugu diocese, the majority attend Mass regularly; each Sunday, Mass is said three times. Even those whose faith has been shaken by suffering are drawn to this place, seeking to find the peace that has eluded them. From the very old to the very young, they pray and sing and thank God for his faithfulness.

When a healing service follows Mass, the crowd waits silently as Fr. Ubald, a bald figure in thick glasses and white vestments, silently processes among the crowd, holding in the air the Eucharist contained in an ornate monstrance. The people draw back, making way for him as he passes, blessing first one then another with the Real Presence. "Jesus. Look at Jesus. It is Jesus who wants to heal you."

If you were to meet Fr. Ubald on the street in America, you would likely see nothing remarkable about this

People gathered at the Center for the Secret of Peace on Lake Kivu

Our Lady of Love

soft-spoken, gentle man. And he would be the first to agree. "God is the one who heals," he says, over and over. "It is my job to be a good shepherd, nothing more." Among his own people in Rwanda, however, he preaches tirelessly and with great conviction about the power of God to heal, and the necessity of forgiveness for those who seek that healing.

You would never know, looking at him, of the nightmare Fr. Ubald has endured. His dark eyes peer out kindly from behind the thick lenses. And yet he is a warrior of mercy who has brought the Spirit of Jesus back to his country.

A SHORT HISTORY

Rwanda, the "land of a thousand hills," is a landlocked country in central Africa roughly the size of Maryland, with a population today of about twelve million inhabitants, having doubled its population since 1995.

The ethnic and political unrest of the country can be traced back to 1916, when Rwanda was colonized by the Belgians, who in the 1940s issued identity cards dividing the Rwandan people into three ethnic groups based on arbitrary

Fr. Ubald during a healing service

factors such as livelihood and physical appearance: Hutu, Tutsi, and Twa. The Hutu comprised the majority and were primarily farmers; the Tutsi raised cattle, and the Batwa[1] lived in the forests. However, over time the issue of ethnicity increasingly created resentment and division, particularly between the Hutu and Tutsi.

At first the colonialists gave preference to the minority Tutsis, giving them the best jobs and educational opportunities, and raising up a group of intellectuals who soon yearned for independence. As colonial powers eroded, the government began to support the Hutu majority in order to widen the divide between the two cultural groups. Hutu forces, supported by the Belgian government, gained political and military influence.

The ethnic and political unrest continued after Belgium granted Rwanda independence in 1961, then worsened under Hutu presidents Grégoire Kayibanda and Juvénal Habyarimana. Fr. Ubald's father and other relatives were murdered in an uprising in 1963; ten years later, Fr. Ubald and his brother were forced to leave minor seminary[2] and flee to Burundi, where they completed their undergraduate seminary studies.

On November 28, 1981, Our Lady of Kibeho appeared as "Mother of the Word" and warned the visionaries of the impending genocide. At this time, Fr. Ubald was completing his seminary studies, working closely with the Legion of Mary, an apostolate focused on prayer and service to the Blessed Mother that had greatly influenced his own mother's spiritual journey. He was ordained in 1984 and took up his first pastoral assignment at Nyamasheke parish, where he spent the next ten years of his life praying for people and teaching them to receive God's healing love. In 1987 he began to pray with people who were in need of healing, and in 1991 he received the gift of knowledge from God,[3] so, as Fr. Ubald says, he "could better serve the people and serve God." He began to travel the country with his message of healing and forgiveness.

In 1990, the Rwandan Patriotic Front (RPF), a predominantly Tutsi group living outside Rwanda because of the ongoing conflict between the Hutus and Tutsis, banded together to win the right to return to their homeland. When

Shrine of Our Lady of Sorrows in Kibeho

peaceful negotiations were resisted by the Hutu government, the RPF took up arms. This was the start of the Rwandan Civil War, which escalated when the president's plane
crashed in 1994, launching a hundred-day wave of violence
by Hutu extremists that ended with at least one million Tutsis and moderate Hutus killed, wiping out whole families,
and decimating the Christian community. This is what is
known as the Rwandan genocide of the Tutsi people.

VOICES OF THE GENOCIDE

"Historical clarity is a duty of memory that we cannot escape. Behind the words 'Never Again,' there
is a story whose truth must be told in full, no matter
how uncomfortable."
                    Rwandan president Paul Kagame, April 7, 2014,
                            Kigali Genocide Memorial Centre

"So many people died at that time," said Fr. Ubald. "It was
as if we were in another world. There were no tears—tears
came later. In the moment we were just wondering who
was next. It wasn't until I was in the Congo that I had time
to cry." It was there that he was reunited with his sister,
Pascasie, whose husband and daughter were killed, but she
herself had miraculously survived and continues to work
with Fr. Ubald at the center. His brother, Révérien, also survived; today he is a policeman for the Rwandan government
and works to reconcile and bring justice to communities torn
apart by the genocide.

LEFT TO TELL

Since the 1994 Rwandan genocide, dramatic stories have
emerged cataloging the violence suffered by Tutsis and the

moderate Hutus who tried to save their friends and neighbors from the slaughter. In 2004, Immaculée Ilibagiza published *Left to Tell*, recounting the miracle of her own survival. In 2009, Immaculée invited Fr. Ubald to the United States not just to share his story but also to preach the message God gave him to proclaim: of the healing power of forgiveness to turn enemies into brothers and sisters in Christ.

Wherever he goes, Fr. Ubald offers a simple yet urgent message to those he encounters in his homeland and around the world: *forgiveness makes you free.* Free to be healed. Free to find peace. Free from the chains of hate and fear. God is the author of all miracles; he is the one who heals. But we must open our hearts and prepare ourselves to receive that healing.

The story Fr. Ubald shares, here and in his preaching, is shocking in both the extreme violence he encountered and the extreme grace that was necessary to restore the peace in his heart. As you read this account, ask God to speak to your heart about the areas of your life that are in need of healing or that you have made "out of bounds" to God. Know that there is nothing—nothing at all—that is too hard for God. There is nothing—nothing at all—you can do to put you beyond the reach of God's mercy.

Even if you have never experienced the kind of unrelenting violence that is described in Fr. Ubald's story, there may still be something that is keeping you from opening your heart fully to God. Let this book speak to your heart. Take it to Jesus in prayer, at church or by yourself at home, and tell him about the things that are holding you back from forgiving that person who has wronged you or from asking for forgiveness. Don't you want peace? Don't you want healing?

Fr. Ubald says, "You must open the door to your heart so that Jesus can come inside and bring peace and healing. This door unlocks only with the keys of forgiveness and mercy."

HOW TO USE THIS BOOK

This book consists of eight chapters. The first seven chapters tell the story of the genocide and the healing and reconciliation ministry God called Fr. Ubald to bring first to the people of Rwanda and then to other parts of the world. The eighth chapter contains a special message to you from Fr. Ubald, a prayer exercise that will guide you, step by step, to the peace and healing you seek. Don't be afraid. God will meet you where you are.

Periodically throughout the book you will find features titled "Voices of the Genocide" that provide historical or cultural context from a variety of perspectives that enhance the story. At the end of each chapter you will also find a section with scripture-based reflections and questions from Fr. Ubald, to help you apply the story to your own life.

The final part of the book is intended as a special resource for parishes and other groups that have been deeply affected by racial tensions and violence. The Mushaka Reconciliation Project outlines, step by step, the process by which former perpetrators of violence have been reconciled with their victims and the family members of those victims. This facilitator-based program, based on Catholic moral teachings, has been used in parishes and secular groups all across Rwanda and in other parts of the world. The appendix offers an overview of the program; for more information, go to Fr. Ubald's website at https://frubald.com.

Finally, a one-hour documentary called *Forgiveness: The Secret of Peace* is available if you would like to share Fr. Ubald's message with your parish group or other study group. You can order a copy of the film at www.secretofpeace.com. This is also the best place to get more information about his travel schedule and how to invite him to your parish.

Heidi Hess Saxton

1.

THE NIGHT OF THE SWORD

And this is the verdict, that the light came into
the world, but people preferred darkness to light,
because their works were evil. For everyone who
does wicked things hates the light and does not
come toward the light, so that his works might not
be exposed. But whoever lives the truth comes to
the light, so that his works may be clearly seen as
done in God.

—John 3:19–21

THE BEGINNING OF THE END—DECEMBER 1963

"Close the door when I leave," my father told my uncle,
twelve-year-old Deogratias, who was living with us. "Do
not open it again until morning. I am not sure that I will be
back." He could smell death.

I was sleeping, so I did not see him go. And I never
saw him again. That night, my father, his brother Juvenal,
and many other members of our family were killed. Horror swept the village, leaving widows and orphans with
nobody to take care of them. I was only seven years old; my
brother Révérien was five. My mother was at the hospital
with my three-year-old brother, John Baptist, carrying my
three-month-old sister, Pascasie, on her back.

When we woke up the next morning, my brother and I
ran out into the yard to play, screaming and laughing. Suddenly our grandfather came straight to us with a lance in

hand, wild with grief. His appearance frightened us—we did not understand why he was so angry and had never seen him so distraught. We ran into the house and closed the door.

"Your father has been killed! Juvenal has been killed! Canisius and Callixte have been killed!" On and on, my grandfather listed the names of the victims of that horrible night. Our mother had not been there to comfort us, only our uncle, who was only a boy himself.

At about noon the next day, our mother arrived at home and learned what had happened to my father. I can still hear the sound of her sorrow. She was now a widow, and we were fatherless. I didn't understand what that meant for us at that time. I didn't know what it means to die or why my mother was weeping.

We hadn't seen her for weeks and were so happy to see her. We didn't understand why she wasn't smiling, why she was so sad, so quiet. She had lost her husband forever. But we did not understand what that meant. We were just happy to have her with us again.

Voices of the Genocide

Fr. Ubald's mother is a heroic figure as the widowed family matri-arch. His sister, Pascasie, remembers their mother, Anysie, as a strong and prayerful woman who seldom spoke of her husband. When Pascasie turned eighteen, she asked her mother to tell her about him and was surprised when her mother did not immediately answer. At last she turned to her daughter and spoke.

"'Ubald is built like your father, but Révérien's face is more like his,' my mother said. Then she grew silent again, until at last she looked up. 'Now I need to go see about my bananas.' And she left very

Fr. Ubald's sister, Pascasie

quickly. I think it was hard for her to talk about even that much."

Life changed that night, changed for all of us. Our joy was taken from us as, very slowly, we began to understand the meaning of death, that we would never again sit in the presence of our father, who had simply vanished. We were forced to endure real poverty—no more tea, no more meat, none of the privileges we had known. My father was no longer there to give us these things.

I began to have dreams about my father and told my mother that I had seen him. "No," she told me. "You have not seen him. You will not see him again." It took time for her to convince me that my father was dead. There was no body; victims of the night sword received no Christian burial. In many cases, there were no family members to

Fr. Ubald with his brother Révérien (right)

bury them, because they had either been killed or gone into hiding to escape the slaughter. We never knew where or even if our father had been buried. We spent a long time at home without going to school, for our mother was afraid that those who killed our father could kill us also on the way to school.

In the years following my father's death, my mother was forced to work hard; he had been a teacher, and without my father's salary from the school, it became more and more difficult to survive as a family. Even so, Mother oversaw our education and made great sacrifices so we could stay in school. She also took care of our spiritual education and prepared us for our First Communion and the Sacrament of Confirmation. She herself was an active participant in the Legion of Mary.

In 1970, at the end of elementary school, I chose to go to minor seminary. I thought about becoming a priest. I had been influenced by Fr. Innocent Gashugi, a priest who led a children's music program at school. He taught us songs and was so kind to us.

One day in his homily at a Mass with schoolchildren, he spoke about Jesus as the Good Shepherd; Fr. Innocent explained that, as a priest, he is to be a good shepherd and that Christians are the flock. At that time the Holy Spirit helped me respond to the call to become a priest.

This calling to the priesthood did not come easily for me. When I was ready to take entrance exams to minor seminary, our parish priest decided that I should be deleted from the list because I was the oldest son of a widow. He said I needed to go and help my mother after I finished school. When my mother, who was spiritually discerning, heard this, she went to the priest and persuaded him that it was God's will that I become a priest, though I was her oldest son.

Finally the parish priest relented. He let me take the test for minor seminary.

LEAVING HOME—SEPTEMBER 1970

Though I was a little sad to leave my mother, I was also full of joy. I spent the first two years of minor seminary at Mibirizi parish. One of my uncles, Barthelemy, who was a teacher, accompanied me and showed me the way.

I first arrived at the seminary late in the afternoon, happy to be there at last. My dream to become a priest was going to become a reality. It was a whole new world for me, starting on the first evening when I discovered electric power for the first time; a generator provided electric energy, and there were electric lights inside the church and in the dining room, classrooms, and dormitory. What a surprise!

All of us arrived at the seminary, coming from different parishes of the diocese. In elementary school we had one teacher who took care of the school and taught everything to us. Now we had many different teachers to teach different lessons. It was really an adventure, a new life.

It was a happy time for me. We had a good priest who was rector of the seminary, Fr. Charles Kabaka. He was a good-natured man who impressed me so much. We prayed, studied, and played together; that was our daily occupation. The secondary school fees were expensive, but I knew my mother was a hard worker and never imagined she might have trouble paying them. It was a happy time of my life. But that happiness did not last for long.

THE SWORD FALLS AGAIN—FEBRUARY 1973

I had just completed my second year of studies when I moved to St. Pius X in Nyundo in 1972, which was about ten hours north. My brother Révérien joined me there when the St. Aloys seminary was closed. The roads were bad, and travel was expensive, but we did not worry about that so much. We left the financial concerns to our mother, who still needed to feed our brother and sister. How would she find travel money for our trip home for Christmas holidays? We did not know. She worked hard, selling banana beer and other articles from her harvest. And somehow, we had money to travel home for the Christmas holidays.

It was to be our last Christmas Day together in Rwanda.

The following February all Tutsi students were chased away from schools by Hutu students. It was horrible! What violence! The same thing was happening in all secondary schools across the country. We had thought that because we were good Christians, in minor seminary preparing to become good priests, such violence could not happen to us.

We were wrong.

One Sunday after evening prayer, the older Hutu seminarians prepared to chase all Tutsi students from the seminary grounds. Older Tutsi students fled the campus, most of them taking refuge in the major seminary or at the bishop's house.

For some reason the younger seminarians were spared, and we stayed quiet that night as we went and slept. The next day the older Tutsi seminarians were sent home, but the younger seminarians were permitted to stay. The priests thought that because we were young, we could stay quiet and study. But that is not what happened. Once the older Tutsi students were gone, the hatred of the Hutu students turned upon us. In the middle of the day, we Tutsi seminarians fled to the major seminary, arriving tired and hungry.

Later that afternoon, the sister who worked in the minor seminary kitchen arrived with food for us, and we were piled in classrooms around the major seminary. Then, at three o'clock that afternoon, three young men we did not know entered the seminary, brandishing machetes and screaming at us, full of hatred.

We were afraid. We hid under desks, and one brave man, a major seminarian and deacon named Ruzindana Didace, approached the intruders and tried to convince them that those who had fled to the major seminary were too young to concern them and that the older ones had already left. Those young men looked at us with fury, and after a time they left. But we knew we would not be safe for long, that most likely the men would return under cover of darkness.

That evening the priests took us to a secret place inside a diocesan storeroom. There were no beds, but it did not matter. None of us slept that night. A band of Hutus—seminarians and local tribesmen—attacked the seminary again that night, but they did not find us where the spies had reported us to be. Once more we narrowly escaped death.

It was not safe for us to remain at the seminary, and the rector—a sympathetic Hutu priest named Monsignor Matthieu Ntahoruburiye—did what he could to get us safely home. One Tutsi major seminarian, Epaphrodite Kayinamura, had broken his leg while fleeing the attack, and so early in the morning the rector of the minor seminary, Fr. Charles Kabaka, rented a great truck to drive us all home.

As we neared Kibuye, we found that a bridge on the road had been destroyed, forcing us to walk the rest of the way. We loaded our trunks on our heads and began to walk.

At the Kibuye parish, the parish priest, a Tutsi named Fr. Sekabaraga, was afraid to help us and urged us to move on, fearing we would be exposed to greater danger from the government soldiers living near the prefecture. He gave us some water to drink, and we went on, arriving at Mubuga parish later in the evening, famished and exhausted.

At Mubuga, the parish priest, Fr. Kayumba Simon, was not there, so we waited for him, thinking he could rent a car to drive us home. Later that day we learned he had been arrested and put in prison in Cyangugu prefecture for helping some Tutsi people escape the violence.

At about three o'clock that afternoon we heard a truck arrive and saw it was full of young people, armed with swords. Thinking it was Hutu seminarians who had pursued us, we fled and ran in every direction—some toward Lake Kivu, others to the bush. In the panic and commotion, I lost Révérien.

A group of us fled once more to the next neighboring Kibingo parish. The pastor, Fr. Innocent, had been my music teacher in primary school, and his life's witness first encouraged me to become a priest. He welcomed us and prepared food for us to eat. We were so hungry! After we had eaten, he showed us where to sleep, and in the morning after saying Mass with us and feeding us breakfast, he blessed us as we set out for home. He was at my ordination in 1984, and he died of diabetes during the genocide, unable to get to the hospital for medical help.

The nightmare continued as we finally neared our village. Wherever we went, people screamed at us mercilessly, as if we were criminals. Hutu tribesmen had set up roadblocks everywhere, and we knew that if we were discovered they could kill us. We walked all day, looking for a safe route home, and when night came we slept in the bush after crossing the Mwaga River.

Early in the morning we stood up and went on. I arrived at the home of my mother's brother at about ten o'clock that morning. He gave me food, but I had not had food or water for an entire day and night, and I swallowed with difficulty.

I did not know where my brother was, and I dreaded going home to my mother without news of him. When I arrived at home at about one o'clock that afternoon, my mother met me with horror and fear in her eyes. "Where is your brother?" she asked me.

I told her that Révérien had been lost when fleeing from the attack of Mubuga parish. And when he finally arrived home late that evening, my brother told us he had hidden in the bush near Mubuga parish as Hutu students from Shyogwe secondary school chased the Tutsi students away from Mubuga's secondary girl's school. Only after the Hutu students had gone had my brother dared set out for home.

"It is not safe for you here, either," my mother told us, her face lined with fear. She was afraid our Hutu neighbors would kill us or see our presence as an invitation to drive us all from our home. Finally she agreed that we should all flee south to Burundi with our uncle Barthelemy. He was a primary school teacher facing prison time, simply because he was Tutsi.

FINDING GOD IN BURUNDI—APRIL 1973

We left in April, my mother and uncle, my brothers Révérien and John Baptist, and my little sister and me. Around Christmastime, after a coup d'état in Rwanda's capital city of Kigali, my mother's brother sent a message to us: "There is peace in Rwanda now—come back home." And so my mother and John Baptist returned to our home at the Karengera Commune in Mwezi parish, leaving my sister in Uncle Barthelemy's care. My mother needed to work the land or there would be no money for us to live on, so she went back to plant the beans and corn and to harvest the bananas.

Révérien and I arrived at the minor seminary of Kany-osha in Burundi, in the Bujumbura diocese, and met many other seminarians from all over Rwanda. We were all to be lodged there before being transferred to different minor seminaries all over the country.

We left Kanyosha in September 1973, so grateful to the rector, Fr. Nkanira, who had found places for us in other secondary schools when there were no more places in minor seminaries in Burundi. Years later, after the 1994 genocide, all the former seminarians who had been hosted by Fr. Nkanira had returned to our homeland and invited him to visit us in Rwanda, to thank him for his hospitality.

Once I had completed minor seminary studies, it came time for me to choose whether to continue graduate studies at the major seminary or to leave and pursue another course of study. I had thought seriously about going to medical school, and I had continued high school studies in minor seminary only because my spiritual director, Fr. Bihege Laurent, told me that it would be easier for me to get into medical school at university if I first completed my undergraduate course of studies. So I stayed, though for some time I was unsure about becoming a priest. I had experienced so much loss, so many bad things; my faith was in crisis. I did not spend much time in prayer, only what I was obliged to do as part of my seminary studies. But slowly, over time, God changed my heart.

THE ROSARY OF MY LIFE

One of the people God used to change my perspective was a seminary classmate named Nasar Kibuti. One afternoon, as we were running back to the dormitory after a football game, Nasar shared with me how he always felt happy after playing football. "I take a shower and then, fresh and healthy, I go to the chapel to pray the Rosary before it's time to do homework," he said to me. His words surprised me so much that I had to stop running. He stopped too. "What's wrong? Are you all right?"

"Does everyone pray the Rosary in seminary?" I asked him. I honestly had no idea! I confessed to Nasar that I never prayed a Rosary on my own.

"Are you serious?" he asked. I nodded. "In that case, you don't belong in seminary." Nasar explained that seminary is a school of prayer, where priests are formed in a life of prayer. As I listened, I found myself become more and more angry. No one had explained this to me! I had no idea that prayer was an essential part of the life of a priest.

Our discussion grew more and more heated. Other seminarians gathered around to listen to us. Most of them supported me, and Nasar's point became lost as he was shouted down—not because he was wrong but because we were all screaming at him, calling him a hypocrite. We were so sure that seminarians who spent a lot of time in prayer did so only to impress the faculty with their piety. I was in seminary to learn—not to pray.

Nasar walked away, his head down as though he was ashamed. I headed for the shower room, proud and self-satisfied. I had won the argument. Nasar and his seminary friends were hypocrites. I was sure of it!

Each time I saw Nasar in the days that followed, my joy slowly eroded, and I became troubled by the idea that perhaps Nasar had been right after all: to be a good priest is to be a man of deep prayer. I tried to chase the idea from my mind, but it was not possible. Finally, I went to spy on Nasar, to see if he really went to the chapel after each game—or if he was the hypocrite I suspected he was. I went inside and saw not only Nasar but also about thirty other seminarians, all praying the Rosary silently and earnestly.

Convicted, I knelt along with them—and realized that I had forgotten how to recite the prayers. After a moment or two, I recalled the Hail Mary and recited it ten times. But I could not recall the mysteries or any of the other prayers. How embarrassing! Everything had been erased from my mind. Not knowing what else to do, I began to meditate on my own life, on the moments in my life that I had experienced God's mercy. Original mysteries!

My First Mystery: Joyful Childhood Memories of My Father

My father was a teacher, an educated man who was well liked and respected; my family was rich, yet he was kind to everybody. Every day I would follow him to school, so proud and happy. Every evening he made us pray together as a family. I thought of him dancing at wedding feasts and laughing with my mother in the dining room at home. We had been so happy.

One day people in our village came to help my father build a new kitchen. At the end of the workday the workers received banana beer, sharing the bottles from one person to the next. Only one man did not get the bottle. He was Mutwa.[1] No one—Tutsi or Hutu—wanted to drink with him. So my father gave me a bottle and sent me to share my beer with that man. I thought it was an honor—one whole bottle of beer, for just the two of us! Amazing!

But my uncle only laughed at me. "Now the other children will not want to share with you or play with you either!" And he was right. But I didn't care. Neither did my father. He did not want me to be prejudiced against anyone. He had already felt the blows of such injustice.

One dark night in 1961, when I was just five years old, my mother grabbed me and fled into the bush, my little baby brother strapped to her back. She had heard the Hutus were taking up clubs and knives against the Tutsi men of our village. And so she left my middle brother with a Hutu neighbor and ran for safety.

My father was savagely beaten when the Hutu men came looking for him. He could not run. He was beaten until he could no longer walk. As his body slowly recovered, my mother massaged his legs until he was well again and could walk with me to school.

All these things I remembered as I prayed. *Holy Mary, Mother of God, pray for us sinners now and at the hour of our death.*

My Second Mystery: The Night of the Sword

I was just seven years old, and yet I could clearly recall the night, just two years later, when all the Tutsi men of my village, including my father, were killed. There was no mercy, only hatred and fear.

That day I became fatherless, and my mother became a widow. My family became poor, and my mother struggled to feed us. Her faith in God never wavered. But it was the beginning of the way of the cross for me.

I was the first to become aware of this new reality, of what it meant to go on living without my father. We didn't eat meat or drink tea because we had no money to buy them. My mother had to cultivate the earth with her own two hands as she could not afford to pay anyone to help her. And yet somehow she took care of us and helped each of us to grow spiritually; she was part of the Legion of Mary and devoted herself to prayer and service in addition to her duties at home.

Holy Mary . . . pray for us.

My Third Mystery: The Banana Robbers

My family was brought still lower one night after my father's death when thieves cut our banana plants and took the fruit. My mother had depended upon this crop as an important source of our family's income.[2] I remember listening to my mother weeping in the night. She could not jump up and defend our property. If she tried to resist, those who killed her husband might kill her as well.

I was powerless too. I was still a child and not a man. I could not defend her then—and I could not help her now that she had returned home. Although I was not yet fully grown, I was old enough to be considered a threat by some, and so my very presence at home would have drawn unwanted attention. I could not help her in any way. I could only entrust her to God.

Holy Mary . . . pray for us.

My Fourth Mystery: My Mother Was Assaulted

As I continued to pray, a scene came up in my mind that I had nearly blocked out until that moment. Once more I saw him: the man who came in and refused to go home, determined to force himself on my mother. I saw my mother fighting him and chasing him out of the house.

Imagine the humiliation, enduring such an insult at the hands of the very people who had killed her husband! That day I experienced the mercy of God, who delivered my mother from her attacker. And yet, the pain of the injustice still burned inside me. This, too, I had to offer to God. Earnestly I turned once more to the Blessed Mother, who during her lifetime had seen her own Son unjustly beaten and killed.

Holy Mary . . . pray for us.

My Fifth Mystery: The Money Basket

In a way, this memory was the hardest to bear, for I had played a part in my mother's suffering. In September 1972, my brother and I were about to return north to minor seminary. I had seen that my mother was struggling to support us. Then, as we were about to leave, she brought a basket to the table. Inside was all the money she had earned over the summer—just a handful of coins. "We must decide how to divide the money," my mother said.

Slowly I took out the money for my school fees (then about thirty-five dollars a year), and my brother did the same. Next, we took out the money to pay for our travel. I could see my mother growing more and more anxious as I looked inside the basket once more. There were just forty francs, about ten cents.

Forty francs, to feed my youngest brother and my sister and herself.

Forty francs, to pay the rent and tend to their other needs.

It wasn't nearly enough. And yet we needed this money too. We had to buy lunch on our way back to school—my brother was too young to go hungry. So we took that money too and left our mother empty-handed and weeping. She sold the family goat to survive. (We had cows until 1960, when our enemies beat my father and killed and ate our cows, leaving us only with the goat.)[3] She was afraid to ask for a loan, afraid she would be assaulted when she was unable to pay it back. There was no bank, no reserve.

It was a scene I shall never forget, that remains with me to this day. My mother's courageous faith became part of the foundation on which my priestly vocation rests. I saw that she was willing to do whatever was necessary—even selling the family goat—to ensure that we her sons could follow our call.

Holy Mary . . . pray for us.

VOICES OF THE GENOCIDE

When he entered major seminary, Fr. Ubald received a sponsorship for his education and living expenses from Karlau parish in Graz, Austria, through a program hosted through the Vatican's Pontificate Missionaire.

Fr. Ubald visited Austria for the first time in 1987, where he met the Schröttner family. In 1988, Mrs. Schröttner came to visit Rwanda, and she met Fr. Ubald's mother at that time. After the genocide, when Fr. Ubald returned to Austria to rest and grieve, Mrs. Schröttner took him aside and offered these comforting words: "I will be your mother to you now."

FAITH RESTORED AND RENEWED

While meditating on these events, I became tormented, thinking of all my mother had endured to take care of us. In reality, I concluded, it was actually God who had taken care of us. Though I had lost my faith, he had taken care of my family.

I knew my mother was a woman of prayer; she had been engaged in the Legion of Mary, a spiritual movement that is strong and dynamic in Rwanda. I was convinced that the Blessed Virgin Mary had helped my mother in her struggle, and after my experience in the seminary chapel, meditating upon the mysteries from my life, I decided that from then on I wanted to pray the Rosary every day. But to do that, I needed help—I needed to learn again how to pray the mysteries properly.

I went to see my spiritual director, Jacques Guillot. I revealed to him the truth about my life, about how weak my faith was and about how I wanted to begin with a new spiritual life. I asked him to write down all the original mysteries of the Rosary so I could pray them each day.

Praying the Rosary helped me to rediscover God's great love for me and my entire family. Through the prayers of my mother, God took care of all her children. I began to thank and praise God for his great love for me. And it was out of that gratitude and thanksgiving that I finally decided to be a priest, to offer him all that I am and to serve him.

My family had suffered great injustice at the hands of the Hutu people. My father and other family had been killed, and my brother and I were refugees in Burundi. We were victims of something bigger and more powerful than ourselves. But this, I could choose. I could choose to offer my life to God.

I began to think about what kind of priest I wanted to be. I knew that one day I would return to Rwanda to preach God's love. Even at the seminary, many people's hearts had not yet been fully converted and were full of hate and fear. We had heard about God, but many of us had not yet encountered Jesus in a personal way.

It wasn't until I escaped with my brother to Burundi and began seminary studies there that I came to understand what it meant to be a good priest and to devote myself to prayer. A friend encouraged me to pray the Rosary each day, just as my mother had. My heart became converted, and I became a true son of Mary.

RETURN TO RWANDA—JULY 1978

In 1978, I returned to Rwanda from Burundi to study in the major seminary. My brother Révérien remained behind in Burundi, where he attended university after completing his studies at the seminary. He became a soldier and was fighting with the Rwandan Patriotic Front (RPF) when Kigali fell.

I was ordained in July 1984 and was assigned to Nyamasheke parish, in the diocese where I had been raised. There I tried to preach love and live love. In 1987, I began to pray for people, and people would return and tell me that they had been healed. I continued to pray, and in 1991 I received the gift of knowledge from God—a gift that enables me to hear God's voice, telling me who he has healed—so I could better serve the people and serve God.

On the evening of April 7, 1994, I was packing to go preach at a mission in the north part of the country. Just a few days before, I had gone to visit my mother. All my family was together; we packed thirty children into the back of my truck and took them for a little drive. I was so happy, shouting, "Are all these children from our family?" It was such a happy time, a happy memory that has stayed with me.

It was the last time I would ever see my mother. Not one of those children survived. All of them died with their parents in the Rwandan genocide against the Tutsi people.

FROM FEAR TO FAITH

Trauma and loss can cause a great fear that can separate us from God. In the first part of my life, I experienced many deep wounds that, for a time, led to a crisis of faith for me: I deeply grieved the death of my father, the loss of many other family members who had died, and the loss of my home when we were forced to escape to Burundi. I was gripped with great fear, and I found it difficult to talk to God.

At the end of minor seminary, I almost thought of becoming a medical doctor rather than a priest. But when I thought of how God had taken care of my family, I realized I had to be grateful. Slowly, over time, I took small steps of faith that helped me set aside my fears until I could sincerely pray, "God, you have been so good to me, and I have nothing to give you. I give what I have to you and come totally to you." I decided to become a priest so I could speak to those who had suffered as I had. I wanted to preach love to *my* people.

Unfortunately, this message did not bear fruit immediately; although I had labored at Nyamasheke parish for ten years, I could not stop the violence. But over time, when I returned to Rwanda, I began to see the fruit of this message flower and grow as people opened their hearts once more to Jesus.

Those who experience deep wounds of the heart often react with fear, making it difficult to trust in the goodness of God. But when we decide to look for the hand of God at work in our lives, the wounds begin to heal. We can once more begin to see God at work in our lives and respond with faith and love.

The temptation to give in to fear may come back, and we must resist it. When I returned to Rwanda and saw the Hutu seminarians who had been with me before I fled, I refused to allow fear to take over my heart. Instead, I chose to see them not as enemies but as people who had themselves been wounded and who needed this message of love.

Perhaps you have even been tempted to think about how to punish those who have wounded you. I tell you, it is far better to redeem those experiences by embracing them in faith, practicing forgiveness and mercy, rather than to take vengeance. Are you willing to begin this journey away from fear and toward forgiveness?

Reflect

Do your wounds weigh you down, causing you to run here and there for words of sympathy and consolation from others? The comfort that comes from other people is not enough; we need to open our hearts to Jesus and let him minister to our deepest needs.

When Jesus was carrying his Cross, he saw the women crying and told them, "Daughters of Jerusalem, do not weep for me; weep instead for yourselves and your children" (Lk 23:28). I believe he did this to show them he had already overcome the wounds that had been inflicted upon him.

Do you have wounds that need to be healed? Are you ready to invite Jesus into those wounded places so you might receive spiritual and physical healing from him?

Have you inflicted wounds on others? Is there someone from whom you are afraid to beg pardon? Jesus taught us, "Therefore if you bring your gift to the altar, and there recall that your brother has anything against you, leave your gift there at the altar, go first and be reconciled to your brother, and then come and offer your gift" (Mt 5:23–24).

We cannot open our hearts to Jesus with faith until we have let go of the burdens inside of us, burdens of fear, vengeance, and shame. Tell Jesus that you want to put those on the altar too. Then take the first step of mercy, whatever that may be for you, toward the one who has wounded you or whom you have wounded. A first step can be something as simple as praying for that person. That is mercy and forgiveness in action. If you are unsure of what steps to take, you can talk with your pastor, counselor, or another trusted, mature mentor.

If reaching out directly to the one who has harmed you or whom you have harmed is not possible, perhaps you can show mercy to someone who has experienced a similar trauma as you, or to a family member of the person you harmed. In any case, you can continue to pray for this person and ask God to show you what you must do.

Are you allowing evil to conquer you by holding revenge in your heart, preventing you from seeing the goodness of God in your life? Scriptures remind us, "Do not be conquered by evil but conquer evil with good" (Rom 12:21).
    In what area of your life do you have a tendency to want vengeance? Are you willing to release this over to God, so your heart can be fully open?

Are you afraid to acknowledge your need for healing? Are you too embarrassed of what others will think if they knew everything about you? You do not need to be afraid, as the beloved apostle reminds us in his gospel: "For everyone who does wicked things hates the light and does not come toward the light, so that his works might not be exposed. But whoever lives the truth comes to the light, so that his works may be clearly seen as done in God" (Jn 3:20–21).

Are you caught in the shame of the evil things you have done in the past? Do not let the evil one trap you. Evil loses its power when the light of Christ shines upon it. God's grace is available to us through the sacraments, in the confessional, and simply by spending time with Jesus in prayer. When we reveal our wounds to the Lord, we can be confident that he sees our need and meets us where we are. Standing in his light, we do not need to be afraid of the darkness.

2.

Blood on a
Thousand Hills

Hear, Lord, and have mercy, for you are a merciful
God; have mercy on us, who have sinned against
you: for you are enthroned forever, while we are
perishing forever.

—Baruch 3:2–3

April 7, 1994

I was preparing to travel to preach at a parish in the north
when my assistant rushed in. "Bad news. The president is
dead . . . plane crash."

It is unclear who or what was responsible for the crash
that caused the death of Rwandan president Juvénal Habyarimana and others. In time, it became clear that plans for the
genocide had been underway long before the crash; this was
simply the catalyst needed to put the plan into immediate,
deadly action.[1] Within twenty-four hours and for the three
months that followed, Hutu extremists stirred up Rwandan
Hutus to take up weapons against former friends and neighbors, systematically killing more than a million Tutsis.[2]

Even on that first night, after hearing of the crash, the
Tutsi people of my parish were frightened that the Hutu
members would respond to the news with violence. There
had already been isolated instances of violence, including a "trial genocide" in 1992 in which hundreds of Tutsi

families were killed in northern Rwanda. Rumors persisted that more was coming. Many were fearful of how the Hutu militia would respond to the news of the president's death.

VOICES OF THE GENOCIDE

"In 1992 I started losing members of my family: my brother and his wife and their seven children were killed in the 'trial genocide.' We later learned that it had been our neighbors who had done this—they had fried the children in oil, and cut off my brother's legs before closing him and his wife inside the burning house. . . . When at last we came out of hiding and learned what had happened, we went to the burgomaster to report them. But he refused to make a report. . . . No one would acknowledge what had happened."

Claudette Mukarumanzi
Genocide survivor

Fr. Ubald with Claudette Mukarumanzi

We had heard rumors that the parish was to be attacked, that the priests were to be killed and the valuables stolen. That night, we priests decided to sleep in the bush next to the parish, Hutus and Tutsis together. We were so afraid, yet we were united. That unity remained until evacuation forced us to go our separate ways.

As we huddled in the bush together that night, we could hear the cries of Gaston Segatarama, the first Tutsi man to be killed near our parish. The next morning I came out of hiding and returned to the church. On the way I stopped by Gaston's house and saw his body; the killers had cut his throat.

The same night at Kibogora, twelve kilometers away, Hutu extremists killed a lady with her two children and wounded her husband, Azarias, and a third child. I visited him in the hospital and saw his family was taking care of him as well as a sick priest, Fr. Augustin. I took the priest home with me to take care of him.

Not long after this, Hutus attacked the hospital. Azarias fled into the bush but was found and killed. His three-year-old son had nowhere to go and stayed at the hospital. Finally a teacher from his school told the boy to come with him to get food. But it was a lie. The teacher killed him. No one survived from Azarias's family. Only his wife and older two children received Christian burials; the others were killed like animals, abandoned in the bush and on the street.

VOICES OF THE GENOCIDE

"In war, men are killed first, because they are the most apt to fight back; the next targets are women liable to help them, and boys because they try to continue the conflict, and then older men who can offer wise counsel. But in a genocide, the killers track down everyone, in particular babies, girls, and women, because they represent the future."

Genocide perpetrator[3]

Sunday Evening, April 10

I went to the police station to ask for protection for the refugees at my parish in Nyamasheke. More than ten thousand of them had come, and there was not enough food and water. The Hutu extremists had cut the water lines to the parish, and we had to ration the water tank carefully. Babies were crying because the milk in their mother's breasts had dried up. All these things I remember; all I must forgive.

Four gendarmes returned with me to guard the parish—four men to protect ten thousand unarmed refugees. They were good men, but it was not enough.

On Tuesday, April 12, all Tutsis were told to go to the parish, where there was greater security for them. That evening the last Tutsis that had been hidden by their Hutu friends arrived at the parish. A Hutu family brought a two-week-old infant whose parents had been killed. "What shall I do with her?" I asked them. "I am a man, I have no milk!" I urged them to keep the baby, to find a new mother who can feed this child with her own. But they refused. No mercy. At last I went to the Sisters of Francis of Assisi, who worked with our parish. They took the baby. I saw her again when she was two years old, so beautiful. She was adopted by a family in Belgium.

Early on Wednesday morning, I received a phone call from the sous-prefect of Rwesero. "The people won't listen to me anymore," he told me. "Take care of yourself; take care of the refugees at your parish. I can't help you anymore." We later learned that he had been working with the militants and the local Hutu people who were ready to begin the slaughter. The holocaust was about to begin, and one poor parish priest could do nothing to stop it. I could only stand with the thousands and thousands of refugees as death came marching toward us.

"FR. UBALD IS A KILLER"—WEDNESDAY, APRIL 13

At nine thirty that morning, a crowd of attackers came screaming, frightening the refugees. The four gendarmes who had been sent to protect us raised their rifles to ward off the attackers. The refugees themselves tried to defend themselves by throwing stones. They wanted to survive. Women and girls gathered stones as the men threw them over the walls.

The gendarmes were good people. They did not want the refugees to be harmed. When one of the perpetrators pushed his way inside, he was shot by one of the gendarmes. "Fr. Ubald has a gun!" the Hutu militants shouted.

Bishop Thaddé Ntihinyurwa

They wanted to stir up excitement, to make everyone turn against the refugees and to hate me. It was a lie, of course. I did not know how to use a gun. Even so, the rumor spread: *Fr. Ubald is a killer.*

I called my bishop, Bishop Thaddé Ntihinyurwa, and told him that Nyamasheke parish was under attack. His house was nearly two hours south of us, but he said he would see what he could do. I exposed the Holy Sacrament in the chapel, where we priests and religious made adoration. We prepared to die.

The bishop arrived at one o'clock that afternoon, accompanied by Bagambiki Emmanuel, the prefect of the Cyangugu prefecture and commander of the gendarmerie. The attackers stopped their aggression, and the prefect invited them to come to a meeting. They obeyed and went with him, but no one from inside the church was asked to come, to represent the Tutsi refugees.

After the meeting, the bishop approached me, saying that at the meeting, people said I'd had a gun and had shot the attackers. Surprised, I asked the bishop if he believed it, and he said he did not—but that to make peace I should allow the militia to go into my room to search for a gun. I had no choice but to allow it, though I touched the pockets of each of them before they went in, to be sure they could not plant a weapon. One of them had a knife in his pocket, and I took it before he entered the house.

None of the men could look me in the eye, for they knew the truth: the gendarmes had been the only ones with weapons and had shot the intruder. Even so, when they came out of the room they cried out against me, determined to chase me away from the parish. I had been ten years at that parish, and they turned against me. These men declared that I must go, that no one would recognize me as the pastor any longer. Only because I was Tutsi.

I went to my room and took my prayer diary and a few clothes. With tears in my eyes I went and blessed the refugees in the parish. They had come to me as their pastor, and there was nothing I could do to help them. The Ben-ebikira[4] religious sisters decided to drive with me to the bishop's house, for their convent was being destroyed, and the bishop sent me away with a Josephite brother named John Baptist, who also wanted to leave Nyamasheke parish.

Back at the parish, panic broke out. Mothers and children cried out with fear, knowing that once I was gone, they would be killed. They trusted me, trusted that after offering ten years of my life, the killers would not be able to kill so long as I was there.

The bishop did not know what to do, seeing all the women weeping. "Don't cry," he told them. "I will stay with you. If you die, I will die with you." John Baptist, hearing the bishop, decided not to come with me. He would stay with the bishop, sleep at the parish, and come to me at the bishop's house the next day.

He never made it to the bishop's house.

VOICES OF THE GENOCIDE

The role played by clergy—bishops, priests, and religious—in the genocide has been a source of heartache and even scandal, causing thousands of Rwandans to leave the Church. On March 20, 2017, in a meeting with Rwandan president Paul Kagame at the end of the Year of Mercy, Pope Francis acknowledged this failure.[5]

"We ask God's forgiveness for the failures of the Catholic Church during the 1994 Rwanda Genocide and for the hatred and violence perpetrated by some priests and religious."

The next day, Thursday, I went to the bishop's chapel at three o'clock to pray, as was my custom. The bishop came

in and knelt beside me, weeping and with blood on his sou-
tane. John Baptist was dead, pulled from the bishop's car
and killed with two other Tutsi brothers, Br. William and
Br. Anton. Seminarian Evarist Nambaje and Fr. Apollinaire
Mtamabyariro, who were Hutu, saw them killed and told
me that the bishop had tried to shield the men with his own
body. But there had been no mercy.

On Friday, the water tank at the parish was completely
empty, and all the refugees were weak with hunger and
thirst. The attackers came from everywhere, from Nyamasheke and Hanika and Muyange parishes. The Hutu militia arrived from Kibuye prefecture to lend their support to
the attackers. Armed with swords and lances, machetes and
nailed clubs, guns and grenades, and gasoline, the murderous rampage lasted three days, from Friday through Sunday.

"A WAR WITHOUT WIDOWS AND ORPHANS"—APRIL 17, 1994

On Sunday, I called the burgomaster of the Kagano Commune, Kamana Aloys, where Nyamasheke parish was
located, and learned that all the refugees had been killed.
"What kind of war is this?" I cried. "A war without orphans
and widows!"

It was later that same day that I found out that my
mother and my entire family had been killed at the
Karengera Commune. Many years would pass before I
learned the details. I cannot begin to describe the great darkness that enveloped my heart. *Why had God allowed such a
thing to happen, and why was I not allowed to die with them?*

For ten years, I had preached for the conversion of
hearts at Nyamasheke parish and worked hard to bring
renewal and healing. Now the only fruit I saw was genocide.
It was a deep inner wound for me.

VOICES OF THE GENOCIDE

In a June 2018 interview, Straton Sinzabakwira, the burgomaster of the Karengera Commune at the time of the genocide, shared his recollection of the killings within his commune.

"I did not know Fr. Ubald's family, except for Révérien, before the genocide. There were so many people who came to the commune for help because we had the authority to save them. On April 11, 1994, a meeting took place in which I received instructions to kill all the Tutsi outside the commune; those inside were still protected. But on April 17, even those inside the commune were to be killed. The Hutu militia had been trained and organized to do the killings. When they finished killing all those outside the commune, they came to kill those inside.

"I had another meeting with the police inspector, the leader of the militia, and others, and I gave them the prefecture's instructions—all in the commune were to die. The militia killed them, but I gave the order.

"Fr. Ubald's mother was one of those killed. Then the men buried the bodies in a common grave, to hide what they had done.

"I did not do any killing myself. Even so, I am responsible for these deaths. I could have left Rwanda instead of giving the order. I could have said no and been killed myself. I could have helped some people escape. Afterward, all I could do was come forward and say the truth from prison: people died. People need the truth. Even if I say it and am killed by those who were with me, I must say the

truth. I did not have the strength then, but I have it
now. I am not afraid of death. I must say the truth."

In the first waves of the genocide, the Hutus turned
against the wealthy and important in an effort to establish
their own government. But I never imagined they would
ever hate us so much or that they might one day wage the
kind of war against us that spared not even widows and
orphans. I never imagined I would live to see outright
genocide.

I had thought my parish was a good one, alive with the
power of the Holy Spirit. It hurt me to see members of my
own parish—those who had once praised God together—
killing one another. I had known most of these people for
the ten years I had been there, and the sense of betrayal was
immense.

One of the men who had chased me away from the parish was a teacher whose school fees I had paid first through
the parish funds and then out of my own pocket. "He must
go," he had said. "We don't want him anymore."

Fr. Ubald with Straton Sinzabakwira (right)

Finally, it was decided that I should leave. One of the gendarmes, a man named Janvier, escorted me to the bishop's house, several hours away from the parish. The extremists had promised not to kill the refugees if I left, and the bishop felt he had no other choice. But it was all a trick. The next day, every one of them was dead.

"Jesus, where are you?" I prayed every night as I wept and wept; I could not sleep. I felt I had failed as a priest, for I had preached love but the people practiced genocide.

I began to pray. Pray for those who were dying. Pray for peace. Slowly, slowly, the darkness moved away and the light grew brighter. Then I heard God speak to me. "Ubald, if you are chased from one town, go to another. That is the Gospel." I had made a decision to die with my parishioners—but that was my decision, not God's. The people were screaming to put my head on a pike, but Jesus had called me to safety.

The next time I went to pray, God told me to remember the persecution of the first Christians, which led to the spreading of the Gospel. Jesus wanted me to use these experiences to evangelize later.

It was then that I knew my life would be spared. God would make a way.

THE WAY OF ESCAPE—MAY 27, 1994

I stayed at the bishop's house for more than a month, unsure of how long I would survive the genocide. I was not far— only a few kilometers—from the Rusizi River, which formed the border between Rwanda and what would become the Democratic Republic of the Congo. But I knew escape would be nearly impossible, and it was only a matter of time before I was discovered and killed. Roadblocks had been set up by militia in all directions; anyone who was discovered trying to flee was cut in pieces on the spot. Already bodies were piled everywhere, as far as the eye could see.

Then I learned that there was one Hutu militia who was ready to help Tutsi refugees escape across the Rusizi . . . for a price: fifty thousand Rwandan francs.[6] I had no money with me, and going to the bank would mean almost certain death. So from the bishop's house I called the bank and spoke to the manager, Gerard, who was Hutu but was also a good Christian. He agreed to allow me to sign a proxy statement and send someone to collect the money.

He could have refused me. I was Tutsi and had no rights—not even the right to live. His kindness proved that not every Hutu participated in the genocide. Unfortunately, many Hutus who tried to help us paid with their lives.

I sent a Hutu priest to the bank to collect the money and had enough to pay for three other people, who were able to escape with me. One of them was Josee, the sister of the wife of my brother John Baptist. Her husband, Christopher Habiyambere, and their two children were hidden with neighbors when the violence broke out; she later learned that they survived the genocide. Josee was pregnant and in no condition to travel, but she was determined to find safety for herself and her unborn child.

We fled during the night. A Hutu priest led us to the man who was to take us across the river into the Democratic Republic of the Congo. We avoided the roadblocks and had to pull Josee up the mountain paths; it was hard for her to breathe. When we finally arrived at the Rusizi River, we discovered a small boat submerged in the water. All the other boats had been gathered together and watched carefully so that no Tutsi could escape. But this man led us to the one remaining boat, and at about four o'clock that morning, we crossed the river.

The man who arranged our escape died a year later from cancer.

REFUGE IN THE CONGO—MAY 28, 1994

The morning I arrived in Zaire (now the Democratic Republic of the Congo), my first thought was to find my sister and other family members, many of whom had immigrated as refugees to that part of the country in the 1960s, during the war for independence in Rwanda. Josee went to live with members of her family who had emigrated earlier.

I found my sister, Pascasie, with her husband's aunt and learned that her husband and child had been killed (I will write more about that in the next chapter). I stayed with my sister for three days before I went to Bukavu, where there was a house for priests who were visiting or waiting for an appointment with the archbishop. I could not stay there indefinitely, and the vicar-general proposed to me that I should go and help the sisters at a health center about sixty kilometers out of town; they had no one to say Mass for them. I was glad to go, because Jesus had told me that he wanted me to escape in order to evangelize. However, I could not speak the local language, so I preached in French, and Sr. Helene translated for me. After Mass, people came to Sr. Helene and thanked her, saying they had been converted. I laughed and said to Sister, "But it was not you who preached; it was me!"

"Yes, but you preached in French. No one understood you. Me, they understood!" she teased me, laughing with her sisters. It felt good, being able to laugh again after two months of thinking of nothing but the genocide. But soon I would return alone to my room and the dark memories would come flooding back. This went on for a month and a half, from the end of May to July 1994, when I was invited to go to Palermo, France, and made it my intention to go to Lourdes, to see if God would speak to me there.

FROM INJUSTICE TO HEALING

Forgiveness makes us free, though it may take time for the mind to heal from dark memories of the past. If we want this healing, we must reject the opportunity to seek our own justice.

When people refuse to forgive, it is as though they carry the weight of those who wronged them on their backs; this heavy burden makes it difficult to stand tall and to run free. Also, if we refuse to ask pardon from those we have wronged, that same crushing weight falls upon us, shaming us and forcing us to turn our faces away from Jesus.

Forgiveness must be unconditional. Not "I will forgive, but he must do this." Forgiveness with conditions is not forgiveness. Conditions keep the door of the heart closed, closed to the other person and closed to God as well. God cannot bring healing unless the heart is open and free of unforgiveness.

When there is violence, the key to the victim's freedom is in the hands of the offender, who must beg pardon; the key to the perpetrator's freedom is in the hands of the victim, who must offer forgiveness. They need one another for both to be free of fear and shame. When this is not possible, someone must stand in for one or the other—someone who has himself experienced forgiveness and can help others become open through their testimony of God's work in their lives.

Forgiveness always goes hand in hand with mercy. When you show mercy to the one who has wronged you, it opens the door for true forgiveness to flow between you. This does not mean forgetting what has happened. The pain of what you have suffered may rise up again and again, and you must be willing to bear it, even as you acknowledge the wrong that was done. The perpetrator, too, must show mercy and compassion for true reconciliation to take place. Otherwise they remain separated and closed both to each other and to God.

In the scriptures, Jesus gives us a clear message: *Love even your enemies, and pray for them, so that they may be converted* (see Matthew 5:44). Hating your enemy is a temptation that must be resisted if you are to be free; Jesus warned us that "those who do such things will not inherit the kingdom of God" (Gal 5:21).

I've met people who have refused to beg pardon for the killings that took my father and other members of my family. They are now old men, in prison—and yet, if they were to come and beg pardon, I could not refuse. To this day, they have refused to beg for pardon, and I continue to pray for them.

When victims struggle to forgive, those around them can help to bring about reconciliation and justice. After the genocide, at Mushaka parish I met one young woman called Donata, who had heard me speak of forgiveness as a way to freedom. Donata's father had participated in the killing of the husband and several children of a neighbor woman. Only one of the widow's sons and some of her married sisters escaped the genocide.

Donata's father was in prison for his crimes, and Donata said to her mother that she wanted to go and take care of the widow. "This woman is alone, getting water and wood. I must go live with her, to take care of her." Donata's mother agreed to make this sacrifice. "It is my husband who killed her family, and her son is a soldier who cannot take care of her. Yes, you must go."

And so Donata went to help the widow, who decided to allow the young woman to live with her. When her son Alfred came home, he became angry. "How can she come and live here?" But his widowed mother replied, "This girl is a good one. It is the father who killed, not her."

Slowly, over time, Alfred saw Donata's kindness. Every time he came to visit his mother, Donata shined his shoes and washed his clothes. Alfred fell in love with Donata because she had so much love for him and for his mother. Everyone was surprised when he announced that they were to be married. Now they have three children; their oldest son's name is Patrick Mahoro ("Mahoro" means peace).

His parent's marriage is the fruit of my evangelization after the genocide, and I was happy to become his godfather. It was healing for me to see these families joined together—I had been unable to reach those in my first parish at

Nyamasheke; here at Mushaka, the Holy Spirit was helping
my witness to bear fruit in the lives of the people.

No, forgiving is not forgetting, and it is not easy. And
yet, deciding to forgive is the only way to take the first step
toward finding the peace you seek.

Reflect

What does it mean to have justice, when someone who has
harmed us escapes without suffering any consequences?
Those who commit evil don't always suffer consequences
for wrongdoing in this life. And yet, we can experience
peace knowing that God is the source of all justice. In the
book of Proverbs, we read:

> There are six things the Lord hates,
>   yes, seven are an abomination to him;
> Haughty eyes, a lying tongue,
>   hands that shed innocent blood,
> A heart that plots wicked schemes,
>   feet that are quick to run to evil,
> The false witness who utters lies,
>   and the one who sows discord among kindred.
>   (Prv 6:16–19)

Donata (center) with her children, father (left), and mother-in-law (right)

To forgive, then, is to put those who have harmed us into the hands of God, who alone can see and judge both human deeds and human hearts. This is true justice. It is also a reason that we must be quick to seek forgiveness from those we have harmed in any way, and to do everything possible to reconcile with one another and with the Church. "For as you judge, so will you be judged, and the measure with which you measure will be measured out to you" (Mt 7:2).

Have you been as generous with others as you would want them to be with you? Have you been as generous with yourself as you are with others?

Sometimes the quest for justice is twisted in envy and resentment. In Genesis 4 we read one example of this in the story of Cain and Abel. Cain was a tiller of land, while Abel was a herdsman. Cain grew resentful of his brother when the Lord favored Abel's offering . . . and that resentment grew to a murderous hatred (see Genesis 4:8).

Jealousy was often in the hearts of those who committed violence during the genocide, causing Christians to attack former neighbors and friends. Jealousy crowds out love until your brother has no place in your heart. It grows and becomes a kind of hate until we seek to destroy the other person and all that person does. This is what happened to Cain.

And yet, God showed mercy to him, even as he banished Cain for his deeds. "Your brother's blood cries out to me from the ground!" (Gn 4:10). Then the Lord placed a mark of protection upon him (v. 15), so that Cain would have time to repent.

Does jealousy and resentment grow within you? Have you been feeding it day by day, killing your relationship with others and even with God? Will you open your heart to Jesus and ask him to remove the jealousy from your heart?

Do Christians have the freedom to hold a grudge against those who have wronged them? Listen to what God's Word says: "Do not be amazed, brothers, if the world hates you. We know that we have passed from death to life because we love our brothers. Whoever does not love remains in death. Everyone who hates his brother is a murderer, and you know that no murderer has eternal life remaining in him. . . . He laid down his life for us; so we ought to lay down our lives for our brothers" (1 Jn 3:13–16).

Those who do not freely forgive from the heart can never be truly free, just as those who avoid taking responsibility for their actions are never truly free. In both cases, they are dying spiritually, for their conscience continues to accuse them. You can lie to people, but you cannot lie to God, and you cannot lie to your own conscience.

When we continue to pray and continue to be merciful to those who rationalize their actions, we bear witness with our lives to the secret of peace that is found in Jesus. In *Evangelii Nuntiandi*, Pope Paul VI said, "Modern man listens more willingly to witnesses than to teachers, and if he does listen to teachers, it is because they are witnesses" (41). We cannot be witnesses if we take pleasure in the suffering of those who have harmed us (or their families). The fruit of this kind of torture is death, not life.

Have you taken pleasure in the suffering of someone who has harmed you? How can you show mercy to them?

How is it possible to show mercy to someone who does not ask for it? Most of the time, the survivors of the genocide would say to me, "We would forgive, but no one has come to beg pardon." In the Gospel of Luke, Jesus offers the ultimate model of forgiveness to those who were putting him to death: "Then Jesus said, 'Father, forgive them, they know not what they do.' They divided his garments by casting lots. The people stood by and watched; the rulers, meanwhile, sneered at him and said, 'He saved others, let him save himself if he is the chosen one, the Messiah of God'" (Lk 23:34–35).

Jesus himself showed us how to forgive when no one asks for pardon. When Jesus said this, no one was begging pardon. Yet here we see that he made the decision to forgive those who had betrayed them even before they begged pardon. We must be like Jesus, to forgive first even as Jesus has forgiven us. This is to become stronger than our offenders, who are tied up with shame and are under the power of evil. It is when the victims forgive and show mercy that they can chase the power of evil from the heart of the offender.

Are you willing to be like Jesus?

3.

"TAKE UP YOUR CROSS, UBALD"

If anyone wishes to come after me, he must deny himself and take up his cross daily and follow me. For whoever wishes to save his life will lose it, but whoever loses his life for my sake will save it. What profit is there for one to gain the whole world yet lose or forfeit himself?

—Luke 9:23–25

WOUNDED HEALER—MAY 1994

In the Congo, I began to think about my mission. It was difficult to think or talk about everything that had happened. I was so tired, so discouraged. Many of my brother priests had died—more than thirty of them were murdered when the genocide broke out while they were at a conference together at Nyundo diocese. My bishop had done his best to protect us, but once the genocide began, there was little he could do.

So many people died at that time, it was as if we were in another world. Tears came later, as in the moment, we just wondered who would be next. It wasn't until I was in the Congo that I had time to cry. I mourned greatly over all those I loved, most of whom I would never see again this lifetime.

Voices of the Genocide

Today the Center for the Secret of Peace has played a crucial role in restoring the faith of those who feel betrayed by representatives of the Church who failed to live up to the call to love. Why did the Church not do more to stop the violence? In his book Christianity and the Genocide in Rwanda, *Timothy Longman devotes an entire chapter to the response of Christian clergy and other influencers in the days leading up to the genocide. He writes,*

> In the Rwandan case, some individuals and groups within the churches did speak out against the rising violence and the increasing scapegoating of Tutsi. . . . Many priests, pastors, church employees, and active laity helped support the efforts of human rights groups that exposed the ongoing violence. . . . Parish priests and pastors served as important informants in human rights investigations. When ethnic attacks occurred, churches frequently offered sanctuary to those threatened. . . . [However,] a majority of the Catholic priests and [Protestant] pastors . . . were Tutsi, and as such could not take a lead in opposing anti-Tutsi racism without exposing themselves to danger.[1]

My Sister's Story

I was so happy that I had been reunited with both my sister, Pascasie, and my brother Révérien. Pascasie had lost both her husband and her daughter, who was killed before her eyes, as she told me recently:

"I couldn't believe it when I saw you, Ubald. I was so happy, yet I wanted to cry. I was sure none of my family had survived. I was only alive because the killers saw the blood on me from my eleven-month-old daughter, Clarise, and thought that it was mine, that I was dead. The machete hit the back of my child's head, and I fell down into a pile of bodies. They thought that I was dead, too.

"After the killers left, a friend of my husband's found me hiding in Hanika church and told me and four other women to come with him, that he would try to protect us. 'I will try,' he said. 'If you survive, it is God's will, and if you don't, it won't be my fault.' Two of the women's injuries were too great, and they died. Honestly, part of me wanted to die too.

"We moved from house to house, three days at a time, until in May 1994, I had a chance to escape to the Congo. And so when I saw you and heard that Révérien had survived and was living in Kigali, it was like a miracle to me."

When I left for Europe, Pascasie decided to return to Rwanda to be near Révérien. She said, "For three days I walked, trying to get to my brother. When I arrived at his barracks—he was a soldier—at first they told me he wasn't there anymore. But someone found him, and at ten o'clock he was knocking at my door—I was so happy! He was shocked at how thin I had become, but we got in his car, and he bought some Coke and wine to celebrate, and we drove to his house where he gave me some food and a bed. It was the beginning of a new life for me."

Pascasie received training to work at a counseling center for genocide survivors, to help victims work through the trauma. She told me,

"By helping them, I found my own burden was eased. While we were in training, they taught us to encourage people to be strong and to see the value of life. This

Fr. Ubald's sister, Pascasie

was a difficult thing to convince many of the victims, who had already lost so much. But we would pray with people and ask God to help them. I found it gave me strength and a new sense of purpose.

"I met my second husband, Aphrodis, at the counseling center; he had also lost many family members. At the end of our sessions, he told me that I had helped him—that I had saved his life. In 2000 we attended one of the Mushaka retreats my brother Ubald was holding for victims of the genocide and made a decision to forgive. This helped us to be free to start a new life; we were married in 2004.

"It was difficult in some ways, to truly forgive—I never had anyone come up to me to beg pardon. I never knew who it was who killed my husband and daughter, and I never knew what happened to their bodies. But I made a decision to forgive because I knew I needed a new start, a new life, and that this was the only way to get it. One day I hope I will find out who killed my family, so I can forgive them in person. But for now, I have done what I can to forgive and to follow Jesus."

STARTING OVER

Seeing Pascasie again, I found myself challenged to look at my own life through a new lens and to see God's hand of mercy in the darkest moments of my life. During those first months of the genocide, while I was at the bishop's house, I had heard Jesus tell me to remember the Christians in the Early Church. They had faced great persecution, and yet because of their faith, the Gospel spread. *I was saved to spread the Gospel*, I told myself.

And so I began to preach about healing in the Congo, telling people of the living Christ who heals. The people in the Congo had never heard this message—so many of them came to me for healing. But even as I was asking God to heal people, I knew that I also had to be healed.

Early in my ministry, I met Lloyd and Nancy Greenhaw of Renewal Ministries. They had been traveling across Rwanda, evangelizing and teaching about the five keys to healing. They taught that we must use five "keys" to open

Nancy Greenhaw with Fr. Ubald

our hearts to Jesus so that he can enter in and begin to transform us. We must thank God with hearts of faith, we must decide to forgive, we must denounce evil, we must choose to live for Jesus, and we must claim the blessings he wants to give.[2]

I saw that this was what I needed to do. And so once more I opened my heart to Jesus and asked him to guide me through the darkness and pain, the terrible pain of what I had seen and continued to see in others. I thanked him for sparing my life. I asked him for the strength to forgive and resist evil. And once again, I decided to live for Jesus. He had saved me for a purpose: to help others find forgiveness, the secret of peace.

From the Congo, I traveled first to Burundi and then to France as I went on my way to visit Austrian friends. They had sponsored my major seminary studies and had invited me to visit them and take a much-needed rest. During this time, the Holy Spirit continued to speak to my heart, reminding me of all the ways he had been at work in my life up to that present moment and challenging me to see how he had been preparing me all along to take up this ministry of reconciliation and forgiveness.

HEALING AT LOURDES—JULY 1994

The Emmanuel Community in France had learned through their community in Bukavu that I had survived the genocide and invited me to speak to them of the Jesus who heals at their evangelization service in Paris. About five thousand people from all over the world listened that night as I told them what had happened. I was the first, I think, to have spoken publicly about the genocide. I told them of the murder of the Tutsi people in Nyamasheke parish, where I was pastor. I told them about hearing of my mother's murder and choosing to forgive. I spoke of understanding what Jesus meant when he told St. Peter to forgive not just seven times but "seventy-seven times" (Mt 18:22).

That does not mean that my grief had vanished. I went on weeping every night from the pain of my inner wounds. I still could not understand how it all could have happened. But no matter what it cost or how much it hurt, I would choose to forgive.

After hearing me speak, many people came up to me, telling me that they, too, had decided to forgive. It was also after this talk that I called Fr. Karl Thaller, pastor of the parish in Austria that had supported me in seminary. He invited me to go and pray at Lourdes before traveling to Austria. At first I did not want to go. I was too depressed, still grappling with all I had lost. But as he urged me to go to Lourdes, I sensed this was what God wanted. And so I took the train to Lourdes and there spent three days in intensive prayer. I went to the shrine at Lourdes where Bernadette had seen the Blessed Mother, and I went into the healing pools. Then as I walked outside along the Stations of the Cross in the Sanctuary of Lourdes, Jesus healed me.

At that first station, "Jesus is condemned," I heard a priest who was leading the stations say, "Though he was innocent, Jesus was condemned—and he accepted his Cross."

As I looked up at the face of Jesus, an inner voice said to me, "Ubald, accept your cross also." I breathed deeply, and I made a decision to carry my cross as well. I would carry the cross of genocide, the cross of one who had preached love in a parish that had been destroyed by that genocide. It was time to stop weeping and to allow God to heal my wounds so that I could help others who needed healing from their wounds.

From that moment, it was as though light radiated from within me. Long ago I had made the choice to forgive, knowing that it was necessary for me to move on and do what God wanted me to do with my life.

In the years ahead, I would have many opportunities to walk in that forgiveness again, to look into the eyes of those who had so deeply wounded me and forgive and show mercy from my heart. But now, this was something else, a tremendous gift that is the grace of conviction. Perhaps for the first time, I understood what it meant to forgive seventy-seven times without hesitation or limitations (see Matthew 18:21–22). Of course there would be temptations to deny that decision. But I also knew that evil is real and that we must resist it with forgiveness.

After Lourdes I drove to Karlau parish in Graz, Austria, where Fr. Thaller was waiting for me. I rested in his parish, then began the work of evangelization that I knew God had called me to do. I said Mass, and I offered healing prayers; Jesus healed many people. After three months in Austria I was invited back to Paris, France, and then to England, where Jesus healed many other people. Soon I was ready to go home. I had already preached forgiveness and prayed for healing all across Europe. But I knew that my place was in Rwanda, where people were suffering so much from trauma and inner wounds—both those who had killed their neighbors and friends, and those who had survived the killing and were trying to find the strength to start life over again.

Home to Rwanda—January 5, 1995

As I left Karlau parish, I was so grateful to the people there and for Fr. Thaller, who blessed me for my new adventure. I arrived in Kigali early in the morning of January 5, 1995. My brother Révérien was waiting for me, dressed in his military uniform. After his studies in Burundi he went on studying at the University of the Democratic Republic of the Congo and had joined the Rwandan Patriotic Front (RPF) when, in the years leading up to the genocide, they began to fight for the right of Rwandan refugees to come home. His presence made me feel secure; I was still afraid that the violence would break out again. It would take time before I was finally free of this fear.

When I first returned to my homeland after the genocide, I didn't know where to go at first; Nyamasheke parish had been destroyed after they had chased me away, and I didn't know at the time that it would later be rebuilt. My brother drove me to the procure, the temporary house for priests in that area, and we had breakfast together. After breakfast, my brother left to return to his unit. He worked so hard—all the soldiers were working day and night to restore peace and order.

While we were at breakfast, I had a big surprise—I met Fr. Octave Ugirashebuja, S.J. He welcomed me and drove me to the Jesuit Center, where I stayed almost a year, from 1995 to 1996. I am grateful to the members of the Jesuit Center in Kigali, who welcomed me.

I left the Jesuit Center to the College of St. André in 1996, then went to the Emmanuel Community, where I lived until 1997.[3]

That afternoon of my arrival from Europe to Kigali in January 1995, my sister, Pascasie, came and visited me. We spoke for a long time about all she had suffered, the deaths of her husband and child, and the agonies she had faced before rafting across Lake Kivu to Idjwi Island, then on to Bukavu in the Congo. We talked about going to visit our mother's home, to see if anything remained.

Fr. Ubald visits his family's property after the genocide

FIELDS OF SHAME AND SORROW

A short time later, Révérien drove us to our village. Our mother's house had disappeared. It had been completely destroyed; not even ruins remained. Someone had planted vegetables where the house had been, to remove any signs that our family had once been there. This happened in many other places as well—those who had participated in the genocide against the Tutsi people destroyed Tutsi homes and planted over the land, as if to cover up the shame of what had happened. It seemed as if they could not bear to think of their actions, much less how they would answer those who would later come to inquire about what had happened there.

So often this is the first human response to shame—to cover it, to try to forget. We do not want to be accountable, do not want to remember. But the Bible tells us that our sins must be brought to the light if we are to be healed. "Take no part in the fruitless works of darkness; rather expose them, for it is shameful even to mention the things done by them in secret; but everything exposed by the light becomes visible" (Eph 5:11–13).

All our fields had been occupied, planted with beans and corn, ready to harvest. And yet the crop belonged not to us but to our neighbors—those who conspired to blot out even our memory, out of shame. When they first saw us return after the genocide, our former neighbors would not look at us or speak to us, so great was their shame. They had failed to rescue even a child from our family. My grandmother's house, my brother's and my uncle's houses—all of them had been turned into vegetable fields.

I think none of us were ready for reconciliation just yet. They were not ready, and my sister, brother, and I were not ready. Both they and we were closed. It was a time of confusion for all of us. At times like that, it is natural to distance yourself from others, to protect yourself. It takes time to look at reality and to overcome the fear. And we were all afraid—we of them, for the violence; and they of us, that we would accuse them. Only my brother was not afraid, I think; he was a soldier.

RETURN TO NYAMASHEKE

I, too, wrestled with feelings of shame, shame at having failed as a pastor. I had been unable to save my people and had been chased away from my own parish. After the genocide, there was no place for me. I saw this clearly when I returned to Nyamasheke parish and saw that here, too, corn and beans had been planted where Tutsi homes and businesses had once stood, where people had been killed.

I stopped just outside what remained of the church, remembering the first days after my ordination in 1984, before I had been assigned to Nyamasheke parish. I was the first priest ordained from the parish where I grew up, Mwezi parish, in their forty-year history. Mwezi parish is where I was born and baptized and where I had received all my sacraments. I was ordained by Bishop Thaddé Ntihinyurwa, then the bishop of the young Cyangugu diocese; there was so much joy among the people, to see one of their own ordained to the priesthood. My mother was especially radiant, so happy to be the first mother to give her oldest son to God. My friends from Austria, who had sponsored my education, were also present at my ordination; the pictures they took that day are the only photographs that remain of my mother and my family.

According to Rwandan culture, the oldest son is responsible for the needs of the parents, and because my mother was a widow, it was assumed that I would return home to care for her after I completed minor seminary. But my mother had insisted that she wanted me to become a priest if it was God's will. She was deeply devoted to God, and she sacrificed greatly to ensure I completed my studies. My ordination had been a dream come true for her.

My bishop, too, had been happy to consecrate me to serve God and his Church and to preach love and peace in a country that was so divided. My father had been killed simply because he was Tutsi; I was determined to preach and to live love in memory of my father and so many others who had died because of hate.

And so, in September 1984 I arrived at Nyamasheke parish and began a decade of ministry, riding all over the countryside on a motorcycle on loan to me by Fr. Allain, a good and generous priest. He had proposed that I become the chaplain of the local Legion of Mary chapter as well as the Xaveri charismatic group for youth. I had never been involved in the charismatic movement up to that time, and I wasn't entirely comfortable with it. But I accepted the assignment in obedience and did my best to serve them in addition to my other parish responsibilities, helping Christians to grow spiritually, praying with them, hearing their confessions, and visiting the sick.

At first I found it difficult to work with the members of the charismatic renewal group, who believed that the Holy Spirit was leading them to bring renewal to the parish. Misunderstandings arose when their ideas and plans were not immediately and warmly received by the parish priests, but in time I came to see them as the lifeblood of the parish and saw that they loved the Church. I began to work with them to create retreats and other parish programs, and in time I came to see myself not only as their chaplain but also as a member of the group.

It was through this charismatic group that I began to think about the different charisms and gifts that were used to build up the Early Church. The book of Acts speaks of the Holy Spirit working through the apostles, giving them gifts they needed to serve. I saw some of these same gifts at work in this charismatic prayer group, and as we continued to pray together, I experienced new life and excitement in my own ministry. These charisms and gifts began to bear fruit in the life of the parish, drawing young people back into active participation. Jesus was really alive to us as we prayed and worshipped together.

The charismatic renewal group in that parish had introduced me to the living Jesus and taught me how important it was to help people meet him. There were only nine of us, but they were eager to serve God and their faith was contagious. The Holy Spirit used these people to make a lasting impact on my ministry.

And now, just ten years later, they were all gone. I stood in the courtyard where I had been chased from the parish, in the place where I had said goodbye to my parishioners. The women—older ladies as well as younger mothers and their children—had wept with despair. I closed my eyes and remembered the look on their faces as I blessed them before I left.

All of them were dead. By the time the genocide was over, forty-five thousand of my people had spilled their blood. In most cases their bodies were left to rot where they had fallen, without even a Christian burial.

All this I remembered. And I wept.

FROM SHAME TO RECONCILIATION

When I first returned to my home village after the genocide, fear and grief would not allow me to look in the faces of the people who had killed my family. And they could not look at me, because of their shame. We needed time to face reality, and to make the decision to forgive and be reconciled—something that was only possible by the grace of God.

When I returned to Rwanda, it was no longer the place I remembered. People who had meant so much to me were gone. I was a man without a home, a priest without a parish. I had to start over, even as I mourned the memory of those who had helped to prepare me for the task I now faced. There was nothing I could do but thank God for each of them and to entrust them into his care.

Over and over I met people who had committed terrible killings and were deeply ashamed over what they had done. The genocide had been organized by highly intelligent people, but it had been carried out largely by people who were swept up into the violence, unable to resist. They never imagined that they were capable of killing. When I later spoke to them, they said, "I never thought I could do this . . . but I have killed people, deaf to their cries." Those who began the genocide manipulated the others. For those swept into the violence, repentance for their wrongdoing and subsequent conversion was relatively easy.

This was not always the case, however. There were some who refused to acknowledge the crimes they had committed; they felt justified because of ingrained prejudices and wrong beliefs. They were blind to the truth, unable to acknowledge the evil of their violent actions. I would need to talk with them again and again and pray for God to help them to be open to the truth.

One day while I was at prayer for such a man, I remembered Horizana, a blind woman I had heard about while I was chaplain of the Legion of Mary. Because of her blindness, Horizana could not go through the normal catechetical teachings, and so I went to her home to prepare her for Baptism. Sometimes as we walked along together, I would close my eyes and imagine what her life was like. It was a small thing, but I was trying to be merciful by sharing her experience. At night I would pray for Horizana, that God would be very close to her in her pain. Over and over I assured her that she was never alone, that God was always with her. She had such joy at this!

I often thought of her as I encountered people who, because of the genocide, were blind to the reality of God. They needed to hear that God had not forgotten them, that they were not alone in their darkness. This was true for the perpetrators—who could hide from others but could not hide the truth from themselves or from God—and it was true of the victims—who felt lost and alone in their trauma and grief.

At Lourdes, Jesus healed me and showed me that I must bring this message of healing to others. I must teach victims to extend mercy, even before the perpetrator is able to acknowledge the truth. I must tell those who have killed about Jesus, who said, "I am the light of the world" (Jn 8:12). It is his light that melts the shame of past actions; it shines in the darkest places of the heart.

Reflect

Do you sometimes find it hard to talk to God because you think he cannot forgive you from the shameful things you have done? This feeling of separation was experienced even at the very beginning of our existence, when Adam and Eve heard the sound of the Lord God walking in the garden. Adam and Eve hid themselves from God, who then called to the man and asked him, "Where are you?" Adam answered, "I heard you in the garden; but I was afraid, because I was naked, so I hid" (Gn 3:8–10).

So often people stop coming to church because of shame. Others go to church and try to hide their shame so people won't suspect anything is wrong without truly repenting of their wrongdoing or showing mercy to those they have harmed. There are no fruits of repentance in their lives, and the agony in their hearts remains; they stay locked in the trauma of what they have done.

Do you sometimes feel cut off from others, unable to connect with others because you are hiding the truth? This often happens in families with secrets of violence. They feel unsure of themselves, always hold themselves back because of their shame. The shame spreads to other members of the family, to other areas of their lives. Only forgiveness and mercy can bring these wounds to light, so Jesus can heal them. Do you need to ask Jesus to heal your family?

If we ask God to take away our shame, he promises that we will experience new life. "I will give you a new heart, and

a new spirit I will put within you. I will remove the heart
of stone from your flesh and give you a heart of flesh" (Ez
36:26).

There is a man, Anastasius, who for almost twenty
years hid his involvement in the genocide. He had killed
the mother of a woman in his parish, Antoinette, but refused
to reveal the crime to her. When I preached about the need to
beg pardon to find freedom, Anastasius went to Antoinette
and said, "I was the one who killed your mother."

Antoinette had been traumatized during the killings;
her captors had refused to give her water. After the killings,
though she could drink other fluids, she was unable to swallow water. When Anastasius came to her and revealed the
truth to her, after twenty years, she was once again able to
drink water without any problem.

Anastasius's revelation was the start of new life for both
of them. He was no longer afraid of being found out, and she

Anastasius and Antoinette

was able to forgive him. He gave her his son to take care of her. She became his mother, and it was new life for her too.

Do you need to experience this new life in Jesus?

There are times when even highly intelligent people do things in the heat of the moment, or because they are manipulated, that they would not otherwise do. They spend much time and energy trying to explain away their own behavior—but the shame remains. Like the prodigal son they must reach a point when they stop running away and repent of what they have done.

In the parable of the prodigal son, the younger son reaches a place where he stops running away and returns to his father: "So he got up and went back to his father. While he was still a long way off, his father caught sight of him, and was filled with compassion. He ran to his son, embraced him and kissed him. His son said to him, 'Father, I have sinned against heaven and against you; I no longer deserve to be called your son'" (Lk 15:20–21).

The father responds with great mercy, offering his son a new life. God offers this to us as well, if we will return to him. What are ways you need to return to God?

What if it is a family member who has brought shame upon the family, forcing them to defend and protect that person rather than acknowledge the truth? Scripture speaks to this as well: "Now this is the message that we have heard from him and proclaim to you: God is light, and in him there is no darkness at all. If we say, 'We have fellowship with him,' while we continue to walk in darkness, we lie and do not act in truth. But if we walk in the light as he is in the light, then we have fellowship with one another, and the blood of his Son Jesus cleanses us from all sin" (1 Jn 1:5–8).

Facing the truth, both to ourselves and others, is the key to breaking this pattern of shame. In Rwanda, I have known priests whose ministry stopped bearing fruit because a family member, parents or even grandparents, had been involved in killings going back for decades. Their children and grandchildren continued to bear the shame and guilt, covered over but not forgotten. When we come to the light and acknowledge the wrongdoing of their family member, Jesus frees us from the effects of the past. Then we can be truly free.

Are there any people you need to seek forgiveness from on behalf of a family member?

4.

MAKING PEACE
WITH THE PAST

I give you a new commandment: love one another.
As I have loved you, so you also should love one
another. This is how all will know you are my disciples, if you have love for one another.

—John 13:34–35

SEEDS OF DIVISION

When I talk about the genocide against the Tutsi people to
those who are not familiar with Rwandan history, I often
hear, "How could such a thing happen in a country where
so many people are Catholic or Christians?"

Yes, how was it possible that a million Rwandan people—from the smallest children to the oldest men—were
brutally murdered by former friends and neighbors, in
fewer than one hundred days? And how is it possible that
so much of the slaughter took place in churches, where the
victims had sought sanctuary? How can it be that priests
and religious brothers and sisters not only failed to protect
those most vulnerable but also in some cases actively participated in the killings?

VOICES OF THE GENOCIDE

This question of why the Church was unable to stop the violence is addressed at length in Christianity and the Genocide in Rwanda. *Timothy Longman writes,*

> Since its inception in Rwanda, Christianity had consistently been, not a faith that preached brotherly love, but rather one that endorsed obedience to authorities, ethnic discrimination, and power politics. When the genocide finally occurred, thus, Christians, including some pastors and priests, felt little or no contradiction between their religious beliefs and their participation in the slaughter of Rwanda's Tutsi.[1]

When a government has been corrupted with injustice, the Church must rise up and stand against evil wherever it arises, and the sooner the better. Unfortunately, seeds of ethnic division, sown by the colonialists who first came to Rwanda, were adapted by the priests and religious who first preached the Gospel. Some of the White Fathers, a religious order that came to Rwanda with the Belgians, asserted that it was better to evangelize the majority Hutu population; others believed that the Tutsis, who were wealthier and better educated, would be more influential.

The Tutsis who collaborated with the Belgians to organize and run the country did influence thousands to be baptized into the Catholic faith. And yet many of these did not experience true conversion. Some wanted the benefits of being connected to the Church. Belonging to the Church opened educational and vocational opportunities that were not widely available elsewhere. As a result, the institutional Church in Rwanda was, from the beginning, embroiled in the same political and ethnic divisions as the rest of the country.

When the genocide erupted, there were many good Hutu men and women who risked their lives to save friends, family, and sometimes even strangers. I might not be alive today if not for some of them. They recognized the injustices that were being committed, and did what they could to save lives.

In the time following the genocide, former friends and neighbors became afraid of one another, afraid to speak of what had happened, for fear of having the violence visited upon them again: the perpetrators by avenging family members, or the victims by an enemy returning to finish the job. Even among moderate Hutus, there was great fear that those who committed the evil deeds would kill anyone who might be able to give witness to what they had done.

How could they make peace with the past? How could they ever rebuild their communities and live in peace? Only by convincing those who had done wrong to come forward, admit what they had done, and ask forgiveness—and by persuading those who had already lost so much to extend mercy to those who had harmed them—could reconciliation take place.

As those in exile, both Tutsi and Hutu, returned to Rwanda after the genocide (nearly a million Tutsis who had been living abroad returned in that first year alone), people on both sides often did not want to speak of the horrific events of the past. Many were fearful that the violence would erupt again. Hatred and suspicion continued to poison people's minds and close their hearts to one another. It would take a miracle to bring about true and lasting peace.

I knew that God was calling me to proclaim his message of forgiveness and healing and to call the people to open their hearts to Jesus once more, so he could heal their wounds. I took up this work in earnest at Mushaka parish, where my bishop eventually assigned me after I returned to Rwanda after the genocide.

RESTORING FAITH

When my bishop informed me that I was to be the new pastor at Mushaka parish, I was afraid that I would fail—the parish had many problems, and administration is not my charism. But I had to obey the bishop, and so I went, trusting that Jesus would provide the answers I needed.

At first there were never more than twelve people in the small chapel each week. So many had lost their faith because of what they had experienced. I spoke of Jesus to the few who were still there, of who he is and that he wants to be with us. I set up eucharistic adoration before each Mass and spent time with Jesus there, staying close to him. One of the parishioners saw me and began to join me at adoration, inviting others to come along. Soon word began to spread that Mushaka had a praying pastor, and the chapel became so crowded that we had to move into the church.

Mushaka parish

Within three months things began to change, and the church became full even at weekday Masses!

When I first arrived at Mushaka parish, I had been warned that there were still ethnic conflicts causing problems at the church. I was the diocesan permanent secretary when a synod was held to examine these ethnic problems and their effects on Rwandan society. It was suggested that I sit down with my parishioners to help them speak openly about their experiences, without fear of retribution, and to discuss the ethnic problems that had destroyed our church and society. And so one Sunday I organized a retreat and gave them a theme to think about and discuss in small groups.

These discussions revealed many common themes: that these ethnic problems were evil; that we all have the same Father and are brothers and sisters in Christ; that we could no longer belong to this or that ethnic group but must all be united; and that in order to do that, we must begin the process of learning how to forgive and to seek forgiveness from others.

Some of the victims of the genocide, including family members of those who had been killed, came with me to the prisons in order to meet their offenders in jail so they could give voice to their decision to forgive. I had taught them that very often it is the victim who must first speak forgiveness in order to give the offender an opportunity to beg pardon. And this is what happened—after visiting the prison several times, we came to the prison one morning and found that the offenders had written letters begging pardon, asking that they be publicly read aloud at Sunday Mass. This opened wide the doors of forgiveness at Mushaka parish.

In the months leading up to 2000, as we prepared for the feast of the Jubilee, the bishop who ordained me, Bishop Thaddé Ntihinyurwa, wrote a letter called "Rwanda: A Dual Jubilee of Hope and Peace," which reads in part, "We live today among the turmoil of a cold war . . . where an atmosphere of permanent precariousness reigns. In this conflictual context, marked by the wounds of history, our path toward the Jubilee of the Year 2000 becomes *hope* and *prayer*. *Hope* for greater justice and peace, *prayer* for the wounds to be healed and for reconciliation accepting to forget the past to build a better future."[2]

The bishop of the Cyangugu diocese, Bishop Jean Damascene Bimenyimana, asked all priests within the Cyangugu diocese to help Christians to forgive and beg pardon in order to celebrate the Jubilee sincerely and with great joy. A special diocesan prayer event was planned, and the bishop asked that there be witnesses from among the people who could testify to the joy that comes from giving and receiving forgiveness. Some weeks before the event, I contacted the bishop and told him that I had three parishioners who wanted to give witness; he suggested that I wait until all the other parishes had been given a chance to respond and then to work with the other pastors to decide which to include.

A few days before the event, I approached the bishop again. I had many more people who wanted to testify. Finally, he told me that no one from any other parish had come forward. I was surprised! I realized that what had happened at our parish, and the process we had gone through to help our members prepare for the Jubilee, had been a unique inspiration of the Holy Spirit—and this plan needed to be shared with others. Over time this program, leading Christians to give and receive forgiveness, came to be known as the Mushaka Reconciliation Project. (See the Appendix for an overview of the program.)

When the Jubilee arrived, it was a joyful feast for most of us at Mushaka parish because of all we had done to rebuild our community and walk the way of peace together. I say "most" because there were still some who were not yet open. Some of the victims were still not ready to forgive the perpetrators, and some of the offenders were still not ready to beg pardon. I continued to hold retreats for both groups and continued to pray that God would work in them.

THE GACACA COURTS

In the years following the genocide, those who had lost their faith recognized that no peace was possible until the full truth of what had happened was out in the open, fully known and acknowledged among all the people. But how could the full truth be told? Most of those who were closest to the events were either dead or were determined to keep the truth quiet.

Immediately after the genocide, when the Rwandan Patriotic Front (RPF) army captured the capital and established a new government, thousands of Hutu families fled to refugee camps in the Congo, in Uganda, and in other nearby countries. But as time passed, many were repatriated to their homeland to find that both the court system and the prisons were crowded beyond capacity. The accused had been waiting for years for their cases to be heard while others whose crimes were just as serious remained free simply because no one was left to accuse them.

Between 2002 and 2012, a traditional form of justice called the "Gacaca courts" was revived to give relief to the overburdened court system and restore a measure of peace to the community.[3] Nearly two million cases were processed through this form of local mediation, in which community leaders listened to testimonies to determine the facts of each case.

While participation in these hearings was voluntary, those accused of crimes who freely admitted what they had done, who asked for pardon, and who were not among those who had planned or led the attacks in the genocide could be released from prison or have their sentences reduced. This encouraged the active participation of those in the overcrowded prisons, where both men and women often remained for years without trial. Frequently, those who had committed crimes were able to identify those who were also involved but had not yet been charged. As a result, victims' families were able to learn the details of their loved ones' deaths. In some cases, the families were able to give the bodies of their loved ones proper burials because of the information they received through these proceedings.[4]

It was at these courts that I met Straton Sinzabakwira, the man who had killed many members of my family, and learned the circumstances of my mother's and other family members' deaths. After hearing his testimony, we drove to former Karengera Commune and saw where the bodies had been thrown after the killings. I prayed for the souls of my mother, my brother's wife and child, my grandmother, uncles, aunts, cousins, and my cousin's children. Then I returned to Mushaka parish, where I was a parish priest, and went on praying for my inner healing.

At another time, I met my brother John Baptist's former friend Kirayi, who had turned away from my brother as he pleaded for help to spare his life. But Kirayi did nothing, and John Baptist was killed simply because he was Tutsi. This was a heavy burden, and I had to fight the temptation to give in to the rage and hate I was feeling. How could his

Fr. Ubald praying at his mother's memorial

friend betray him like this? Why did God not prompt him to spare my brother's life?

In time, I came to see that it was precisely because I had endured this kind of senseless loss myself that I was able to listen to the stories of so many others with compassion and without judgment. So many others died under these circumstances, simply because there was no compassion. This callousness left deep wounds that needed healing as well. And this is the work God was calling me to do.

Voices of the Genocide

"On June 23, 2005, I went to Gacaca near Nya-masheke to give testimony. People from all over the country were there because they had heard of the burgomaster who had confessed to being involved—they wanted more information so they could convince others to do the same.

"Fr. Ubald was a parish priest in that area and was invited to speak. I was seated with the other prisoners. When I saw him, it was as if a heavy stone was taken off my heart. It came my turn to speak, and I said, 'First, I want to give apologies to Fr. Ubald.'

"Fr. Ubald came and embraced me. He said, 'I was waiting for this moment. I knew my family had died, but no one came and said, "I know what happened to your family." I have been waiting for this for a long time. In Jesus' name, I forgive you.'

"Less than a week later, Fr. Ubald came back to the prison to see me. 'I want to show you that I give you pardon, from my heart,' he said.

"In 2017 I finished my sentence, and Fr. Ubald helped me to get back on my feet and start my life over. This collaboration, showing people how to reconcile, has had a powerful effect on many people. Whenever I have a chance to give my testimony, I have a chance to make right in a small way."

Straton Sinzabakwira
Recalling the events of that first meeting with Fr. Ubald

Fighting Fear with Faith

People who knew me before the genocide, particularly from the healing services I conducted in the first ten years of my ministry, would frequently come to me at Mushaka parish to get help with the inner wounds they had suffered in the violence. They would unburden themselves, and we prayed together—this is called "Christian listening."[5] This would often ease the burdens of those who had no other outlet for their pain. After they told their story completely, they were often healed.

One woman came and told me she had no reason to live. "My father and mother have been killed. So have my sisters and brothers." She named her brothers, and I recognized the name of one of them, Evode—he had been a couple of years behind me in seminary. "Even if you have no more family," I tried to comfort her, "stay with the one who loves you—Jesus."

"Jesus!" she cried out. "No! Please! Not him! Where was Jesus when my family was killed?" She cried and cried, and I had to wait for her emotions to subside before I could say anything more. Finally, she grew quiet, and I asked if I could pray for her. Laying my hands on her head, I asked Jesus to make himself real to her once more. Then I asked him to heal her and give her inner peace. The next time I saw this woman, she was full of joy. The night after I prayed for her, she told me, she fell into a deep sleep, and Jesus came to her and healed her.

Not all people were healed instantly; most experienced inner healing over a period of time. One woman who came to my office barely made it into my office and sat down before she began weeping. She cried and cried, and I waited for her. She thanked me from her heart, for it had been the first time she'd been able to cry since the genocide. Then she began with her story: how the militia had killed her husband and four children, then stripped her and led her naked to the roadblock where they intended to kill her. Then suddenly, RPF soldiers rescued her. Now she was living with her mother-in-law, sad that she had not been able to bring even one child along with her. "Really I have no right to be there—this is my husband's family. But all my family was killed. So what can I do?" Her mother-in-law had tried to reassure her that she was welcome, but she could only think of all those she'd lost.

When the woman had finished her story, I invited her to come to the church that Wednesday evening for prayer and to come on Saturday for the Mass with healing prayers. When I thought of her, I stopped and prayed for her.

Three weeks later, the same lady stopped at my door and asked if she could speak with me. I didn't recognize her! She was laughing and sharing with me that after three weeks of praising God and going to the healing services, God had healed her wounds. Praise God!

I was always glad when people came to me for prayer. So many people stopped going to church after the genocide against the Tutsi people. Thousands of people had been slaughtered in churches after going there for sanctuary. This made it difficult for people to connect with Jesus in a personal way. But as people began to come to me and I invited them to open their hearts to Jesus and let him heal them, many of them began to return to the Church.

A Healing Retreat

In 2005, some of the killers had served their sentence and were being released from prison. One morning after Mass, three genocide victims came to me in great distress. "Our lives are in danger!" they said. "The men who killed our families in the genocide were released from prison and arrived here yesterday!" Their faces were drawn with fear, and I invited them to my office to talk with me.

In my office, they repeated the rumors they had heard being circulated about the former prisoners, that they had threatened to return and finish the job so that no Tutsis would remain alive and the genocide would be complete.

As I listened to them, I agreed that they were right to be afraid. And I assured them that I would try to find a way to resolve the problem. I also told them, "There is something that you need to do, if you want to find peace. You must bring your worries to Jesus, who is the only one who can give you peace. Remember when the disciples came together in the Upper Room, after Jesus had died? They were afraid of the Jewish authorities who might come after them too. Then Jesus appeared and said, 'Peace be with you'" (Jn 20:21). I invited them to come to one of the parish retreats, where Jesus would free them from fear of the former killers.

The theme of the retreat was Romans 12:21: "Do not be conquered by evil but conquer evil with good." As we prayed, the Holy Spirit began to work in the hearts of the people who were there as I spoke: "As Christians, we are called to forgive just as Jesus forgave from the Cross. Forgiveness is a great gift, an unconditional gift. We don't forgive because we have no more problems but because we have made a decision to be free of the burden of fear, the burden of hate, the burden of vengeance. Jesus forgave those who had betrayed him, and those who were killing him even as he died. He stayed on that Cross, and he forgave."

I could see they were listening carefully. After I finished preaching, I invited them to sit together in small groups and share about the things that had happened to them. I gave them a few questions to get them started: "What bad things did Hutu people do to you and your family?" "Do you believe all Hutu are bad? Are there any good Hutu?" and "What would you like to say to those who perpetrated the genocide against the Tutsi people?"

One by one, each person spoke of the injustices that had been done to them. They spoke of seeing small children killed before their eyes, of women and girls being stripped naked and abused before they were executed, and of Hutu who had threatened to kill every surviving Tutsi in order to obliterate every sign that they had ever existed. Each person spoke from the heart of their fear that it would happen again, no matter what.

After the last person had spoken, I asked one final question: "Do you want to kill the Hutu, just as they have killed your relatives, your wives, your children? Do you want to do the same to them?"

At this, they shook their heads. It was a big no.

"We are Christians," they said to me. "We cannot let such evil defeat us. We must conquer evil with good, just as the Bible says. But these killers . . . we must pray that God will change them. And we must be merciful to them, so that they will no longer be afraid, no longer want to kill us out of fear."

It was then that I realized they had been listening to my preaching. They didn't want hatred and revenge to take root in their hearts. I promised to announce this message to the people at Mass on Sunday and give the victims an opportunity to deliver this message in their own words.

That Sunday, the Hutu in the congregation were stunned when they heard the message of mercy from the victims of the genocide, hearing blessing and forgiveness instead of denunciation and vengeance. It became clear that those who had been released from prison had also lived in fear, that the families of those they had killed would take their lives in retaliation. They were shocked to realize this was not the case, that their victims were praying for their conversion so that the killing would cease once and for all.

Shortly after the Gacaca courts, the leaders of church communities came together in a meeting and decided that those in Mushaka parish who had participated in the genocide against the Tutsi people should not come to receive Communion for at least six months, until they had received instruction and had fully repented for what they had done. This was necessary to begin building trust within our community, to make it clear that the Church would not turn a blind eye to the deeds of those who had taken human lives.

Now I saw that God had been working in the hearts of former enemies and was bringing us together as brothers and sisters in Christ. When the former killers realized that their former victims had found peace, they came to me and said they wanted their own retreat as well. They and their families had suffered as well, and they were afraid that they could never be forgiven. People had accused them of giving false confessions, of turning in other people only to secure their own release. Many Hutu families had lost everything in the refugee camps and returned to find other families on their lands and in their homes. They did not know what to do. "In the genocide, we were like wild animals!" they said to me. "Now we want to make things right."

This worried me at first, the idea of putting victims and perpetrators together in one retreat. What if the two groups were filled with angry spirits and decided to fight one another? What if this was only a trick?

Then I realized that a retreat would only be possible if we invited a third group. No victim of genocide could have survived unless some Hutu intervened on their behalf. The Cyangugu diocese, where my parish was, is very far from the area where the RPF army had been able to intervene and rescue Tutsi survivors. Any Tutsi survivor must have had someone of Hutu ethnicity to save them.

And so I announced there would be another retreat. I invited the survivors, the perpetrators, and those who had been the rescuers. Together, we would talk about what had happened and ask Jesus to bring us together as a community once more.

COMMUNITY AT LAST

As we gathered the three sides together, I prayed that the Holy Spirit would help all those present to be open to the healing that needed to take place in our community. So many Tutsi people had deep inner wounds and were suspicious of everyone. As far as they were concerned, there was no such thing as a good Hutu. They saw only killers.

I invited the victims of the genocide to stand up. Many of them still had the scars of the genocide: missing limbs and other visible injuries. Then I invited the Hutu rescuers—those who had refused to participate in the killings and instead tried to save lives—to go and stand near those whose lives they had helped to save. "Look at this!" I remarked. Each of the victims was surrounded by six or seven Hutu, who had worked together during the genocide to try to save him or a family member. This was no small thing; it meant risking their own lives if they had been caught. So one Hutu family would hide a victim in their home as long as they could then give him to another family when the militia became suspicious. This went on for three months, until the genocide against the Tutsi was stopped by the RPF soldiers.

"Are all Hutu bad?" I challenged them.

"No," came the response. "Those who rescued were good."

I nodded, and we talked about the difference between ethnicity (which is morally neutral) and ideology (which can be good or bad). Those who killed Tutsis *because* they were Tutsi had been following an evil ideology. But many Christian Hutu had rescued Tutsis instead of killing them. And so, those who had harbored hatred against Hutu because of the violence came to see that their hearts also need to be converted. They, too, needed to start a new life.

The discussions continued, respectful and open. Later, the parishioners of Mushaka parish were called upon to facilitate the Gacaca courts to decide what should be done to those who committed violence during the genocide. Near the end of the hearings, the Christians of Mushaka decided that those who had committed acts of genocide needed the spiritual help they could find at our retreats. And after three months of catechesis, those who had done the killing went to reconcile with the families of those they had killed. In many cases, the widows and orphans at the courts would assure the killers that they were forgiven and plead with them to go for the catechesis, so they could start over with a new life. When at last the catechesis was complete, there was great rejoicing, for like the prodigal, our "brother was dead and has come to life again; he was lost and has been found" (Lk 15:32).

Victims and perpetrators tell their stories at Nyamata parish

FROM ISOLATION TO COMMUNITY

When I was preaching in the prisons, many perpetrators expressed concern about what would happen to them when they were freed. How would they and their children be treated? Would the family members of their victims now try to kill them? They had great fear of returning to their communities. I spoke to them often of forgiveness as a way to begin a new life, denouncing the influence of evil ideologies and prejudices. In many cases, these people were able to beg pardon and be reunited with their communities. However, in some cases evil won.

Satan wants to destroy community; he is a destroyer by nature. He has no love, no mercy. He hides in the shadows, trying to keep people from acknowledging his existence. He entices people to do evil while pretending to be good, like the killers who took human lives while wearing rosaries around their necks. They did not recognize that they were under the influence of evil at that time. They had allowed evil to infiltrate their thoughts, bringing fruits of confusion and lies in their actions.

Parishioners participate in a reconciliation celebration at Ntendezi parish

Evil was at the heart of the genocide, causing people to believe lies about one another, to denounce the truth. This created great confusion over the community. They looked at those around them and saw not brothers and sisters in Christ but enemies, not children of God but animals. They fell into the temptation of evil spirits and gave in to fear and hate. Evil spirits hold some people back from receiving forgiveness, and they need to be released. Evil spirits frequently use unforgiveness to destroy individuals and society.

Those who are trapped in sin and feel as though they can't be forgiven must recognize that they are believing a lie. It may be that pride is blinding them, so that they justify their actions rather than humble themselves and seek help. They must resist the lie and seek healing through the prayers of a priest or other mature Christian who believes in the power of intercessory healing prayer. Prayer combined with believing faith is powerful. It brings healing. Both the person who is praying and the person receiving the prayer must believe. They must ask for the gift of faith.

Thanks be to God, truth is a powerful force for change when we communicate the truth not only with our words but also through the witness of our lives. We must tend to the needs of those who oppose us. We must reach out to raise them up, acknowledge them, and remind them of their own dignity. The simple presence of goodness is a powerful antidote to evil.

And when we find that we have been the victims of evil and are separated from our brothers and sisters in Christ, we must offer the pain we feel to God, allowing him to use that pain to make us more compassionate, more open to the sufferings of others. When we do this, the pain transforms us. When we refuse, we become closed to the work God wants to do in our hearts. Because of his mercy, God works in the hearts of both the victims and those who have committed wrongdoing. "God proves his love for us in that while we were still sinners Christ died for us," (Rom 5:8) the Bible says.

Is there someone in your life from whom you have isolated yourself? Have you built up a wall between you, brick by brick, that keeps you from seeing this person clearly and with compassion? Someone who has betrayed you, lied to you, taken something from you that can never be repaid or made right? Jesus is asking you to make a decision to reject evil and do good.

Ask the Lord to come between you and shine a light so that you can see clearly and with compassion. You don't need to do this on your own. Ask God to show you how to be merciful to this person, in Jesus' name and for his sake. Ask for the gift of forgiveness.

Reflect

In the Gospel of Luke we find a passage that was the guiding principle of the Gacaca courts: "If you are to go with your opponent before the magistrate, make an effort to settle the matter on the way; otherwise your opponent will turn you over to the judge, and the judge hand you over . . . and throw you into prison" (Lk 12:58).

We are to minister justice through acknowledging the truth of what has happened. Is there something in your life on which the light of truth needs to shine? Is there something you have done—or something that has happened to you?

How often do we surrender to a conspiracy of silence, afraid to admit the truth, even to ourselves, of some evil that has taken root within our lives, within our homes, or within our communities? The Bible tells us, "Those who conceal their sins do not prosper, but those who confess and forsake them obtain mercy" (Prv 28:13).

How often are we tempted to leave the confessional with a particular sin still weighing on our hearts? Can you ask the Lord to give you the courage to return, to stand against evil, and to commit to starting a new life in Christ?

If we want to remain free from the power of evil, we must remain connected to Jesus. But for this to be true, we must know Jesus, really know him—not just about him. To remain connected to Jesus is to draw life from him, to spend time with him in prayer, and to be open to the work of conversion he wants to do in our hearts. Jesus says,

> Remain in me, as I remain in you. Just as a branch cannot bear fruit on its own unless it remains on the vine, so neither can you unless you remain in me. I am the vine, you are the branches. Whoever remains in me and I in him will bear much fruit, because without me you can do nothing. Anyone who does not remain in me will be thrown out like a branch and wither; people will gather them and throw them into a fire and they will be burned. If you remain in me and my words remain in you, ask for whatever you want and it will be done for you. (Jn 15:4–7)

To remain connected to Jesus involves more than being baptized and going to church every week. The Rwandan genocide teaches us of the necessity of a true conversion of the heart. Despite claiming to be Catholic, many in Rwanda at that time were living in darkness, influenced by evil. They did not show love or mercy.

Do you have joy and peace in your life? If not, there may be some evil in your life that is chasing it away. Offer a prayer from your heart, asking Jesus to reveal himself to you. Ask him to speak to you as you spend time with him, in adoration or reading scripture during your prayer time.

Examine your life, and ask God to show you if there is any habit or ideology that needs to be cleared away. Read the Bible, not just as a historical account of the life of Christ but also as an invitation to meet him personally.

When you encounter a difficulty, ask Jesus, "What should I do?" Then sit and listen, and wait for him to speak. Many people when they pray, talk and talk and talk, and never listen. Take time to wait for him to speak to you.

When you are connected to Jesus, there will be fruit in your life. You will have peace, even when trouble arises. When you invite Jesus into your troubles, he will guide you along the way of peace.

5.

A HEART OF COMPASSION

Jesus went around to all the towns and villages, teaching in their synagogues, proclaiming the gospel of the kingdom, and curing every disease and illness. At the sight of the crowds, his heart was moved with pity for them because they were troubled and abandoned, like sheep without a shepherd. Then he said to his disciples, "The harvest is abundant but the laborers are few; so ask the master of the harvest to send out laborers for the harvest."

—Matthew 9:35–38

WOUNDED SHEEP

As I prepared for the larger retreat, to bring together all the members of my parish—the victims, the perpetrators, and the rescuers—I found myself thinking back to all I had experienced since the time of the genocide. I asked God to give me a heart of compassion, to help me see how I could be a good shepherd to all my people. Many of my sheep were badly wounded, and I needed to understand them, to have compassion and show them how to get back on the right path. Only then could we begin to set aside the hypocrisy and lies, and begin to live together again as brothers and sisters in Christ.

Some victims are understandably reluctant to forgive or to have compassion on those who had harmed them. Many had left the Church because of the genocide. They had been deeply wounded and could not imagine how it could be right to forgive those who had done so much harm. And yet they also felt the weight of their burdens and would come to me with tears, eager to find relief.

To victims reluctant to forgive, I explain that to refuse to forgive is to carry that person always on your back. The weight becomes heavier and heavier until it crushes you. I tell them, "If you want to die, don't forgive. But if you want to begin with a new life, you must make the decision to forgive. Rwanda is our country, and if we don't want to die, we must find a way to live together. No more Hutu, Tutsi—we are all Rwandan."

So many of my family members, including my parents, had died in violent uprisings in my home country from ethnic and political groups fighting for power. My life had been spared so that I could preach the message that only God can make lasting peace, that forgiveness is the secret of peace. When I returned to Rwanda after the genocide I continued to bring this message wherever I could.

Fr. Ubald meets people in his village

A School of Peace

When I first returned to Rwanda after the genocide, I was initially appointed to be the assistant pastor at Cyangugu Cathedral. It was here that I was assigned two new responsibilities: I was to be the chaplain of the prison and the permanent secretary of the synod on ethnic problems in the Rwandan Church. Both these new assignments paved the way for me to take up this new phase in my ministry of healing and reconciliation. Two years later, I became pastor at Mushaka parish.

Education and formation were badly needed if Christian communities were ever going to be rebuilt. And yet, many regarded the Church and its ministers with suspicion and a deep-rooted sense of betrayal, for it was fellow believers who had taken up weapons against the innocent. In the years following the genocide, many Catholics left the Church—some joining Protestant communities, some converting to Islam, and others losing faith altogether. I began to ask God to make a place for this message of transformation and reconciliation to be heard very clearly. In time, this would be the primary work of the Center for the Secret of Peace.

However, in the years immediately after the genocide, this work began right where I was, at Mushaka parish. People needed to be reminded of their inherent dignity and value in the eyes of God. They needed to see one another as true brothers and sisters in Christ once more if this great evil was ever to be eradicated from our land. They needed to encounter in a new way Christ the Healer, Christ the Redeemer, and Christ the Prince of Peace.

Years later, when the perpetrators came out of prison, I told them, "Because you killed, you can't receive Communion until you have had catechesis for six months, every Saturday." They would come to the classes, and after three months I would say, "Now, go to the families of those you have killed and beg pardon." It was a good exercise, getting the victim and perpetrator to speak to one another. Before

going to meet the widows or orphans of their victims, the
perpetrators were afraid. What would they do or say? What
if they refused to receive the apology?

"If they will not hear you, you must show mercy to the
families. You must find a way to let them know you are sincerely sorry for what you have done." They would visit the
family members in the hospital and bring them food. They
would return property that had been taken from the victims.
They would find ways to serve. By these good deeds, the
victims saw that the one who killed their mother or brother
had changed. The violence that was once inside them was
not there any longer.

Some who tried to beg pardon met resistance from their
victims or their families. These people would return to the
church and ask someone to go with them to the families. It
could take time, even months, but when they finally spoke
with one another, victims would come to me and say, "I'm
not afraid of him anymore. Let him go and receive Communion again." This was how many of the victims of the
genocide have been able to move on and have a new life.

Once these families began to speak to one another
again, this new life continued to bear fruit between them.
They took care of one another. When there was some life
event—when a child was married in one of the families,
for example—they came together and helped one another.
This was true whether the marriage took place in the family
of the victim or the family of the perpetrator. The victims
were the first to help, to show they have really forgiven; the
murderer's family came to help with the feast to show they
have accepted this forgiveness. When Christians have forgiven, we can truly pray without hypocrisy. And God hears
us because there is no hatred or fear blocking our prayers.

Outside the parish, people were amazed when I told
them what was happening among the families at Mushaka
parish. I traveled all around my parish, and beyond, telling
people of the freedom that comes through forgiveness and
showing mercy. I gave witness from my own life, of having

forgiven in Jesus' name the man who had given the order for my family's death. I knew that one day God would challenge me to show mercy to him so that the forgiveness could bear fruit.

But what more could God ask of me that I had not already done?

A Miracle of Mercy

In 2005 I was going every Thursday to the Gacaca court in Mwezi, where I was born. I went back to testify and listen to the offenders. Some were ready to confess and beg pardon, and others were not. Some remained in jail because they refused to admit what they had done.

One of the men I met while doing prison ministry is in his eighties; he had been a teacher with my father. When my father was killed in 1963, this former colleague was a regional representative and one of those who had arranged the killings. He arranged additional killings during the genocide in 1994. Yet he refuses to acknowledge his guilt. Like many extremists, he justifies his actions. If he were to be released, it is likely the killings would continue. In his heart, evil has won.

If you refuse to admit what you have done and beg pardon, you can never be free. Often people who refuse to let go of this burden of unforgiveness or shame become physically sick, and doctors can't find the source of the illness. The burden of guilt and shame can attack the body as surely as cancer cells. But when you release your burden, healing often follows.

I had already forgiven in my heart my family's killers long before I testified in the Gacaca court near my home village. For me, these courts ensured that justice would win. It allowed me to know the reality of what had happened and helped me to see that nothing like the genocide against the Tutsi people would ever happen again.

As I listened to the families of the victims and the perpetrators give testimony, I was struck by how different it was now from when my father was killed. At that time, in the years following independence, his killers showed no remorse, no sense of guilt. They were proud to have killed him and my other family members. They had been rewarded and recognized in society as courageous and had taken the lands and other possessions of those they had harmed. They had killed only the men, allowing the children of the victims to grow up and be a continual reminder of what they had done. And in so doing, they unwittingly planted the seeds of genocide; when the killing began again, this time they freely gave in to the temptation to kill even women and little children so no one would remain to remind them of what they had done.

Thank God, the plans of these evil people did not entirely succeed. And the Gacaca courts were restored to ensure that what had happened would not be rewarded and would not be forgotten. Whenever possible, the possessions of victims were returned to their families. This was not always possible, of course. For example, my mother's home, made of bricks, would have been very expensive to replace (ten million Rwandan francs), and her killer's family was very poor. My brother, sister, and I did not need the home, so we forgave the debt.

For me, this was part of showing I had been sincere when I made the decision to forgive Straton in Jesus' name. Straton Sinzabakwira, the burgomaster who gave the order for my mother and family to be killed, had once been a community leader, but now his position and wealth were gone. He remained in Rusizi prison in the Cyangugu diocese from 1997 to 2017.

While Straton was in prison, his family, including his wife and children, had become very poor. I didn't realize how poor until one day a man came to me, full of news: Straton's wife had died, and his son Enod had been chased from school because they could not pay the school fees. He expected that I would be happy. "What's the matter, Fr. Ubald? Why do you look so serious?" he asked.

I knew what must be done. These children had no more parents, no one to take care of their needs. And so from that day, they would live with their aunt, and I would informally adopt them by making sure they had money for their education. "You must come to me if you need anything," I told Enod. "I will help you."

The following year, their aunt came to me. Straton's daughter, Giselle, had passed her exams and was admitted to secondary school, and there was no money to send her. What could I say? I paid for her schooling. It was painful, of course, to look at them and remember what their father had done. But by caring for these children, showing mercy even beyond the call for forgiveness, they know they can trust me and my family—even my brother, who is a soldier—and don't have to be afraid of us.

The people at the school did not know about our arrangement or why I was paying their fees. The headmaster assumed I was a relative, and so when the children had problems at school, he called me. I learned that the boy, Enod, did not want to study anymore; instead of studying, he wanted to sleep.

I didn't want this to continue, so I invited Enod to come and talk with me. Finally, after we talked together for a while, he told me he was ashamed of what his father had done and couldn't bear any longer to think of the crimes he had committed. He felt that everyone who looked at him was judging him for what his father had done. We talked together for a long time, and I prayed with Enod to forgive his father. And from that day, he went and studied well; today, he is a carpenter.

Giselle did very well at school. When my cousin Assumpta, whose father had been killed in the genocide, wound up at the same school, Giselle looked out for her and took care of her. When Assumpta came to visit me and I asked her about school, she said, "Everyone thinks Giselle and I are sisters." And in a way, they were—for I was caring for them both.

Years went by, and I continued to pay the fees for Straton's children. While I was glad I had been able to help them in this way, I was happy it was almost time for their schooling to be done. But one day Giselle came to me and said, "I've decided I want to be a doctor. Would you pay for my medical school?"

At first I was speechless. It was so expensive, and I had already paid so much! But when I looked at her, so hopeful, I knew there was only one thing to say. "Of course I will pay. And when I am old, you will take good care of me!"

These deeds of mercy and forgiveness are already bearing fruit in the next generations, as children of the victims' families accept without question the children of those who perpetrated the violence. Forgiveness stopped the violence.

FROM HYPOCRISY TO MERCY

After the genocide, many victims spoke of feeling a tremendous sense of betrayal because of the suffering inflicted upon them by former neighbors and friends. After years of taking care of their children, sharing their food, and showing mercy in many ways, it was unthinkable that the neighbor could turn against them with such violence, killing not just men but even women and children. It was the deepest kind of betrayal, and their suffering was increased because it came from the hands of people close to them.

To decide to forgive, or to decide to beg forgiveness, is often very difficult. On our own, it can be impossible. There is only one sure way to find the strength to forgive those who have wounded us, and that is to decide to live for Jesus. Jesus is the one who gives us strength to forgive the impossible.

In the Gospel of Matthew, Peter approached Jesus and asked him, "'Lord, if my brother sins against me, how often must I forgive him? As many as seven times?' Jesus answered, 'I say to you, not seven times but *seventy-seven times*'" (Mt 18:21–22; emphasis added). Jesus did not mean that after seventy-seven times we could stop forgiving. He meant that we must forgive *every time*. I think that to ask Jesus such a question, Peter must have had a problem with forgiveness. "If I have to forgive," Peter seems to be asking, "what is the limit?" He was looking for a way out. But there is no limit to genuine forgiveness. No conditions. No exceptions. Not if we want God to "forgive us our debts, as we forgive our debtors" (Mt 6:12).

It is this kind of forgiveness, and *only* this kind of forgiveness, that will wipe away the last traces of resentment, fear, and hypocrisy so that our prayers might flow freely to God. To set limits to forgiveness is to allow the possibility that someone may one day take up the fight again. This is not how Jesus forgave.

Jesus showed us how to forgive without limits, and he did it from the Cross. "Father, forgive them," he prayed, "they know not what they do" (Lk 23:34). To forgive seventy-seven times is to forgive to the point of death and even beyond that.

After the Resurrection, Jesus offered Peter an opportunity to beg pardon and to receive the gift of mercy and forgiveness. Take a moment and reflect on this passage from the Gospel of John (21:15–19):

> When they had finished breakfast, Jesus said to Simon Peter, "Simon, son of John, do you love me more than these?" He said to him, "Yes, Lord, you know that I love you." He said to him, "Feed my lambs." He then said to him a second time, "Simon, son of John, do you love me?" He said to him, "Yes, Lord, you know that I love you." He said to him, "Tend my sheep." He said to him a third time, "Simon, son of John, do you love me?" Peter was distressed that he had said to him a third time, "Do you love me?" and he said to him, "Lord, you know everything; you know that I love you." [Jesus] said to him, "Feed my sheep."

Notice that Jesus had suffered so much, yet he did not remind Peter of his denial. His focus instead was love: "Do you love me?" Peter must have felt such shame.

When Peter was invited to feed the sheep, this was more than just forgiveness. It was mercy. Jesus made him responsible, showing his trust in someone who had been untrustworthy. This too is a kind of mercy.

Peter knows now who Jesus really is, how much he is really loved. What Jesus did here touched Peter so deeply that he would be willing to die for Jesus. He would no more be tempted by evil or deny Jesus again, having experienced this forgiveness. He decided to live for Jesus, and at Pentecost when the Holy Spirit came upon him, Peter proclaimed Jesus as the risen, forgiving Lord: "You who are Israelites, hear these words. Jesus the Nazorean was a man commended to you by God with mighty deeds, wonders, and signs, which God worked through him in your midst, as you yourselves know. This man . . . you killed, using lawless men to crucify him. But God raised him up, releasing him from the throes of death, because it was impossible for him to be held by it" (Acts 2:22–24).

Peter never again tried to hide the fact that he was a follower of Jesus. He accepted Jesus' forgiveness, and it changed him. He became the one who witnessed to the life-changing power of the Gospel and lived only for Jesus both in his life and at his death.

Reflect

In the final days of his life on earth, Jesus was betrayed and abandoned by those he had loved. Peter denied him three times. Judas betrayed Jesus to his enemies for just a few coins. It is often those who are closest to us who can inflict the deepest wounds, and they are the hardest to forgive.

When Jesus forgave Peter and asked him to "feed my sheep," he was showing the truth of what he had explained to Peter once before, that we must forgive each other "seventy-seven times" (Mt 18:21–22). After the

Resurrection, Jesus showed mercy to Peter by pursuing him, restoring him, and raising him up. He invited Peter to live out that forgiveness by showing *lifelong mercy*. This is where love and justice meet.

Where does love and justice meet in your life? To whom do you need to show the same lifelong mercy God has given to you?

We have said that to live for Jesus means to give up our own ideas of justice and to entrust the person who has wronged us to God. And yet in the Gospel of Matthew we read, "You have heard that it was said, 'An eye for an eye and a tooth for a tooth.' But I say to you, offer no resistance to one who is evil. When someone strikes you on [your] right cheek, turn the other one to him as well" (Mt 5:38–39).

"An eye for an eye." Does this sound like vengeance to you?

In the Old Testament, Moses witnessed terrible violence—one person killed would result in the loss of many, many lives. "An eye for an eye and tooth for a tooth" represented a *limit* to the penalty that could be exacted. It was a form of mercy. And yet in the New Testament, Jesus extended that mercy still further. "Do not resist. Turn the other cheek. Offer no resistance to evil."

We are not to cooperate with evil, and we must avoid the one who is evil by helping him to change. After the genocide, people who had helped to organize the killings were put in prison to protect society from further violence. This was a form of justice, and a society without justice is disordered. But we would also go into the prisons to help them change because justice is also needed to fight evil. Justice tempered with mercy.

How do you think Jesus is asking you to temper justice with mercy today?

Do you struggle with hypocrisy? Are you claiming to forgive, yet your heart remains closed to the person you have supposedly forgiven? Consider this passage from the first letter of John: "We love because he first loved us. If anyone says, 'I love God,' but hates his brother, he is a liar; for whoever does not love a brother whom he has seen cannot love God whom he has not seen. This is the commandment we have from him: whoever loves God must also love his brother" (1 Jn 4:19–21).

When we cover over our proud or uncharitable thoughts with generous deeds just so others will think well of us, this is a form of hypocrisy. This is what Jesus was pointing out when he taught his followers that God looked with greater pleasure on the widow's small offering than on the large donation of the Pharisee (see Mark 12:41–44). Similarly, in Matthew's gospel we read, "Take care not to perform righteous deeds in order that people may see them; otherwise, you will have no recompense from your heavenly Father. . . . But when you give alms, do not let your left hand know what your right hand is doing, so that your almsgiving may be secret. And your Father who sees in secret will repay you" (Mt 6:1, 3–4).

How have you seen this principle at work in your own life and in the lives of those around you?

The apostle Paul is a good example of the heart converted with mercy that made a decision to live for Jesus. As a Pharisee, Paul (then Saul) reacted with violence toward Christians until he encountered Jesus on the road to Damascus (see Acts 9). Blinded by a brilliant light, he received healing and a new name through the same Christians he had persecuted. And so, Paul wrote in the letter to the Romans, "'If your enemy is hungry, feed him; if he is thirsty, give him something to drink; for by so doing you will heap burning coals upon his head.' Do not be conquered by evil but conquer evil with good" (Rom 12:20–21).

This verse has helped me in many retreats I have preached. By doing good, we can begin to change our society and be witnesses to the power of Jesus to change lives and heal our deepest wounds.

6.

Stories of
Eucharistic Healing

"When Simeon prophesied over the infant Jesus, he said to Mary, 'Behold, this child is destined for the fall and rise of many in Israel, and to be a sign that will be contradicted . . . so that the thoughts of many hearts may be revealed' (Lk 2:34–35). This redeeming work of Christ continues wherever his name is proclaimed, where he is a 'sign of contradiction' among those who have turned away from the truth. And yet, many people will find hope and healing, if they allow the message of forgiveness and mercy to move in their hearts."

—Immaculée Ilibagiza,
phone interview on June 6, 2018

NYAMASHEKE PARISH, SEPTEMBER 1984

As part of my duties as a newly ordained priest, I was assigned in 1984 to be chaplain of the charismatic renewal movement in the Cyangugu diocese, in which Nyamasheke parish was located. This was years before the genocide against the Tutsi people, and yet God was already preparing me for the work of forgiveness and reconciliation I would be doing after the genocide. He knew how many people would need these healing prayers, how many would need to be drawn back to Jesus after suffering so much pain, fear, and sorrow.

In 1987, an outbreak of bacillary dysentery broke out in my parish and killed many people. I had to go to the hospital to anoint the sick, but at first I was afraid of catching the illness. "Don't be afraid," the doctor said to me. "As long as you wash your hands after touching the sick, you should be fine." I was still afraid, but I went to the hospital and found forty sick and dying people in a great room. One of the women who died soon after I anointed her was a member of the Legion of Mary, and so we carried her body to the church for burial. As I said Mass for her, I thought, *If the doctors don't know how to stop this disease, we must ask God to stop this calamity!*

I invited parishioners to pray for the sick people at the end of every Mass. And after a month or two, the dysentery was gone. Was it because of the doctors, or because of our prayers? I didn't know. But a new sense of vocation was rising up within me. I knew that my people needed to meet Jesus the healer. And so I gathered together eight or nine young people who wanted to pray for healing for others, charismatic Christians who wanted to serve God and his people. (Sadly, most of them died in the genocide.)

We began to pray for sick people in the small chapel parish priests used for their morning and evening prayers. In that small chapel, Jesus manifested his glory, power, and mercy to his people. At first we prayed privately for people who we knew needed healing, without knowing whether or not the healing had taken place. But as people returned from their doctors, claiming they had been healed, we praised God with them.

One day in June 1991 we were praying together in the chapel after Mass, thanking God for his mercy on the sick. Everyone was quiet when suddenly I had a vision of a foot coming toward me, moving like a snake. It scared me! Then a voice told me that someone's left foot was suffering wounds that would not heal. The vision disappeared. Next I saw a face, and the voice told me that someone was suffering from dizziness. I saw a chest, and the voice said someone was suffering from a heart attack. One after the other, I saw these visions and the voice continued: Someone had elbow pain. Another was unable to sit because of a wound on his buttocks. A pregnant woman who had been infertile needed reassurance that she would carry her child to term. Finally, the voice told me that someone there was wondering if it made a difference if he prayed or not.

This was all very new to me. Tentatively, I asked if someone's left foot was sore. A woman raised her hand. "Is someone suffering from dizziness?" I asked. A man raised his hand. One by one, most of the healings had been claimed, with just a couple of exceptions. Over time, many—including the woman, carrying her healthy infant—would witness that Jesus had healed them. Together we gave thanks to God—and I urged them to confirm the healing with their doctors if they had not already done so.

One Hutu woman, Mary, had been embarrassed to admit that she couldn't sit because of the wound on her buttocks. She was ashamed to claim the healing! But afterward she came up and told us, thanking God with us that it had been completely healed. Jesus had healed her spiritually as well. Years later, during the genocide, she brought bananas and sweet potatoes to feed the Tutsi refugees at the parish. She had experienced the love of God and was determined to show that love to others.

Another woman hadn't claimed her healing because she didn't recognize herself by my description at first. "I didn't think I was infertile because I had already given birth to two children!" she said to me. But her next two children had died in the womb, and the trauma of losing those children caused her to become infertile for the next seven years. But she wanted another child and asked the prayer group to pray with her. When she became pregnant, she became afraid that she would once more give birth to a dead baby. When a short time later she gave birth to a healthy child, she brought the child to me, full of joy that Jesus had heard her prayer and healed her womb.

Later that summer we had a series of charismatic retreats at Nyamasheke parish. At the end of each retreat we would invite people for healing prayers. Many people were healed at these services, and they went away telling everyone they met that Jesus is alive and heals. Because word was beginning to spread, I decided I needed to inform the bishop of what was happening at the parish. I went to visit Bishop Thaddé Ntihinyurwa, who encouraged me to continue, reminding me of the story of the apostles in Acts 3:1–10, when they healed the paralyzed man in the name of Jesus. He advised me not to continue praying in the chapel in secret but to begin praying for people in the main sanctuary of the church. I did this for the first time on September 28, 1991.

It was such a joy for me to lead people close to Jesus the healer. Although God had given me the gift of knowledge, to know their wounds, I knew that the healing itself always comes from Jesus. As a priest, it is my job to bring Jesus to the people. As God continued to heal people through these prayer services, I sensed that God wanted me to evangelize in other parishes, and so I went to see the bishop to receive his counsel and blessing. Soon I was receiving invitations from all over the diocese from people who wanted to meet Jesus the healer.

LONG-DISTANCE HEALING

In a short time, word began to spread about these healing services, and I began to receive invitations from outside my own diocese. In the archdiocese of Kigali at the Jesuit Remera Center, Fr. Christian (who was also active in the charismatic renewal movement) invited me to come and pray with the people after the afternoon Mass. Jesus healed many people that day, and I later discovered that he had healed at least one person who was not there at the time! A lady who had been suffering greatly from back pain had made a painful two-hour trip to attend the service at the Remera Center. She and her husband had already exhausted every medical solution. She had gone to Europe for treatment, and when the doctors there could do nothing for her, she returned to Rwanda and sought treatment from Rwamagana Hospital, which specialized in Chinese medicine. They treated her with painkillers but could not correct the problem.

When she heard of the Mass with healing prayer that was to be held one Sunday afternoon at the Remera Center in Kigali, she and her husband decided to attend the service. On Sunday morning her husband took the car and left, promising to return in plenty of time to take her to the service that afternoon. As the hours passed and he did not return, she became more and more anxious. At two o'clock he still had not returned, and she laid in her bed and cried. She had come all this way for nothing! She could not walk that far, so she sent her friends to the center to go and pray for her. And they did.

During the service, Jesus visited this woman in her sick room and healed her.

At the center, as it came time to announce the healings so people could claim the blessing God had given to them, I was prompted to announce that Jesus had healed people with back problems. Some with back pain raised their hands, praising God for the healing—including the woman's friends, who didn't realize that, right at that moment, God was healing their friend as well! It wasn't until they got home that they realized what had happened. When they arrived, they found her on her bed, complaining that her back was burning, with sweat pouring down.

"Get up! Jesus has heard our prayer! He has already healed you!" they said to her. She stood up from the bed, and they sang and praised God together. This woman was at Mass the next day to give witness to her healing.

All these things took place in the years leading up to the genocide. For almost ten years I preached within my diocese and all across my country about Jesus the healer. I saw so many people receive physical and spiritual healing. I saw relationships healed and families reconciled. I saw many people open their hearts to Jesus and decide to reject evil and live only for him. Sadly, many of these people died in the genocide—while others gave in to the fear and hate that brought the genocide Our Lady, while weeping many tears, warned us about at Kibeho.

It was only after the genocide that many began to listen and respond to Our Lady's message. In 2009, I met Immaculée Ilibagiza, who also survived the genocide and went on to tell her own story in the bestselling book *Left to Tell*. She had been traveling all over the United States, telling her story, and had published a book about Our Lady of Kibeho in 2008.

In 2009, Immaculée invited me to come and speak with her and bring healing prayers to the people in the United States. Since that time I have been coming to America twice every year for several months.

It has been such a blessing to see God bring physical and spiritual healing to so many people who have opened their hearts to him. I have invited some of them to share

Immaculée Ilibagiza and Fr. Ubald

their stories here, to encourage you to open your heart to Jesus and receive healing from him too.

I Prayed for My Daughter; God Healed Me (Chicago—October 2016)

As told by Heidi Saxton

I first encountered "faith healing" while I was still an Evangelical Protestant. During that time I had witnessed what appeared to be authentic healings. Unfortunately, I had also witnessed some excesses that made me skeptical about the authenticity of whether these kinds of miraculous healings are truly from God.

After I was confirmed Catholic in 1994, I decided to get a theology degree at Sacred Heart Seminary in Detroit. In one class, I asked my professor to explain how "faith healing" fits with the Catholic teachings on suffering. He explained that the Sacrament of the Anointing of the Sick is intended to strengthen the mind, spirit, and body of the seriously ill for whatever was in store—whether immediate physical healing, suffering, or the life to come. "Sickness, like other forms of human suffering, is a privileged moment for prayer, whether asking for grace, or for the ability to accept sickness in a spirit of faith and conformity to God's will, or also for asking for healing."[1] He also said that healing prayers (faith healing) have a place within the Catholic tradition, though he admitted he had never seen it himself.

My professor's explanation helped me to keep an open mind, and so when I first met Fr. Ubald and heard of his healing prayer ministry, I was cautiously interested in finding out more. At one women's retreat in Minneapolis, I saw Fr. Ubald pray with people for the first time. I was struck by his peaceful, quiet spirit and the fact that he repeatedly directed attention not to himself but to Jesus.

Since then, I have had the chance to witness a few of his healing services in which he processed with the Eucharist in an ornate golden monstrance around the sanctuary, blessing people with the presence of Christ. Afterward, he would go to the front and have someone translate for him what he had heard from God. Then he would ask people to come forward to claim their healings and give witness to what God had done for them. Whenever this happened, I was struck by his repeated attribution of the healings to Jesus and by the specificity of the healings. "Someone's left ear has been healed." "Someone has broken a relationship because of a lie. God wants you to be reconciled." "Someone has prayed for years for her husband with ALS. God has healed him." Each time, someone came forward to claim their blessing, and others who had been healed in previous services came to testify that, yes, they had been healed as well. It was a moving—and often sobering—experience.

In October 2017 I decided to bring my daughter to one of the prayer services. My husband and I adopted her and her brother when they were young, but the effects of early childhood abuse and neglect still troubled them. After Mass, Fr. Ubald processed through the sanctuary and everyone knelt—everyone but me. I had been unable to kneel for several months due to severe pain in my knees, residual effects of a car accident years prior. Instead, I sat in the pew with my daughter's head in my lap, praying quietly for God to heal her.

"Please, Jesus," I prayed. "Please heal her and heal our family." She stirred and sat up, looking around to see what was going on as I continued to pray. At some point, I shifted my position so my head rested on the pew in front of me. And as I heard Fr. Ubald pass my pew, I looked up and realized that I was *kneeling without pain*. What a surprise! I hadn't been able to do that in months.

After the service, Fr. Ubald prayed for my daughter, and we are trusting for her healing. But from that day to this, I have not had any trouble with my knees, and it is wonderful to be able to kneel in church again!

MY LITTLE BOY WAS HEALED OF CANCER (CHICAGO—JANUARY 12, 2017)

As told by Karen Brogan

On January 12, 2017, my husband and I learned that we were facing the fight of our lives. Our four-year-old son, Marty, had been diagnosed with a rare form of cancer called rhabdomyosarcoma. Now the cancer had spread to his lungs, stage IV, and he was facing forty-three weeks of chemo and forty-three rounds of radiation.

Shortly after we received this diagnosis, we heard of Fr. Ubald and of the Mass with healing prayers that was to be held at a nearby church, St. Gerald's in Oak Lawn, Illinois. My family and I attended the service in March 2017 with a picture of Marty and drank in every word Fr. Ubald had to say. At the end of the service, I was disappointed when Fr. Ubald did not mention that anyone with Marty's symptoms had been healed. Others went up, claimed their healings, and gave testimonies of having received healings in prior services. It was amazing—but I could not understand why my son had not received the healing we'd asked for.

"You must have faith," Fr. Ubald said. "You can't just come one night and think that's it. You must be an active participant." And so that night started my spiritual journey. I began to attend church every Sunday and go to adoration and pray the Rosary every day. I began going to Confession and praying daily. I thanked God for all the good in my life and begged God as well as Mary and all the saints to cure my son of cancer. As a family, we began to pray together at home for God's healing and protection. Our faith grew stronger and stronger.

As I continued to pray for my son, I felt great inner peace. Somehow, I felt, everything would be okay. When Marty got his next scans in August 2017, the MRI and CT scans showed that Marty's tumor was shrinking.

To our joy, we found out that Fr. Ubald was coming back to the United States right before Marty's November scans, so this time my husband, Patrick, and his whole family went to the healing service in Kankanee, Illinois. Patrick brought a picture of Marty and the shirt Marty wore to all his scans. Fr. Ubald blessed the picture and the shirt.

However, when we received the results of the November scans, we were confused when the MRI and CT scan showed that the tumor was the same size it had been in August. We had believed that Marty was healed. But it had not grown, and this was a hopeful sign. And on January 12, 2018, the PET scan confirmed that the tumors were dead, and Marty's oncologist confirmed that he was in remission. Our prayers had been answered! Marty was cancer-free. And we believe that he had been healed for a long time—it just took science some time to catch up!

I am so incredibly thankful to Fr. Ubald and to God. Of course, God healed my son, but he sent Fr. Ubald to me and to my family to help us come back to the faith.

God Tackled the Pain of My Son's RSD (Aiken, South Carolina—October 23, 2013)
As told by Ernesto Barquet-Gonzalez Sr.

My son Ernesto Jr. played football for the junior varsity team since his freshman year at Aiken High, until his foot was injured on September 28, 2011. The initial sprain generated a nerve problem called reflex sympathetic dystrophy (RSD), which "locks" the nerves so that they kept signaling pain even after the initial sprain is healed. His foot became hypersensitive, and he could not tolerate the slightest touch. The condition put a lot of strain on him as well as our whole family.

We tried nerve blocks and other procedures, which only alleviated the symptoms slightly and for a short time. Finally, after going to many different doctors and specialists, we were told that RSD is incurable and would likely worsen over time. Even the vibration of a car or plane outside was enough to set off his pain. We were told that Ernesto would be in a wheelchair for the rest of his life.

Ernesto refused to give in to this and fought to keep up with his schoolwork and to get around with a cane as much as possible. He never lost his faith. We found another specialist in Greenville, South Carolina, who attempted to ease his pain by administering shots twice weekly for nearly six months. We heard about a therapy that would mask the symptoms of the pain. This meant Ernesto had to wake up at four o'clock every morning to undergo three hours of therapy in order to get to school by eight o'clock. Then after school and homework, he had more therapy until he went to bed at eleven o'clock at night. This continued for all of 2013. Still, the pain never entirely went away. But neither did his faith—Ernesto heard God say to him that he had plans for him and that one day he would be healed.

On October 23, 2013, we went to Greenville in the morning for Ernesto's shots, then came back to Aiken in time for the Mass and healing prayers at our church with Fr. Ubald. I had heard of this priest's gift for healing, and I knew this would be an important moment in our lives. When Fr. Ubald went forward to mention those who had received healing, he said, "A boy who has had a lot of pain in his left leg has been healed." He asked whoever it was to come to the front—and Ernesto walked forward, without even a cane! He had no more pain. From that moment, he no longer needed any kind of therapy. Two weeks later, he ran a 5K. He can now move without pain and sleeps undisturbed.

Ernesto is a warrior who fought this physical challenge with God's help. Ernesto knows he is a living testimony of God's love and power, and we rejoice that God heard our prayers, healed our son, and gave us new peace of mind.

A Sister Story (Green Bay, Wisconsin—September 25, 2014)

As told by Cleopatre McCormick

First, I should say that I was never a fervent Catholic. I always found reasons not to attend Mass or Confession, and I would fall asleep during the Rosary. Sometimes I would even forget to say grace before meals! One day in September 2014, a friend who listens to Relevant Radio called to say that Fr. Ubald was going to be at Our Lady of Good Counsel Shrine in Green Bay, Wisconsin. My sister and I made plans to go with our babies—she had a three-year-old in need of healing, and I had a one-month-old daughter who battled acid reflux and constipation.

When we went, I was wearing a wrist brace because of severe pain in my wrist. I was shocked when Fr. Ubald said someone with pain in the wrist had been healed. I didn't go up at first—I was sure it couldn't be me! Then he said it a second time, and sure enough, it *was* me! Ever since then my wrist has felt great, praise our merciful God! Over time, our children regained their health as well.

A year later I went back to the shrine for another healing Mass, and another sister of mine was healed. I sensed that she was being healed as Fr. Ubald approached with the Holy Eucharist; I was praying for her and all the other people who had come for healing. She told me later that she'd had the same feeling, that she was being healed. She was too shy to testify, but at my next opportunity I went up and gave witness to what God had done for our family.

Today my daughter is perfectly healthy and is very energetic, and I have grown in my faith after seeing God's healing work in the lives of my family members. God is marvelous indeed!

BREATHING FREE (JACKSON HOLE, WYOMING—DECEMBER 29, 2015)

As told by Cathy Loewer

I once thought that believing in God was a sign of weakness. Now I believe just the opposite is true. It's easy to hold a grudge; it's easy to believe in the things we can see, touch, hear, and feel. It takes courage to have faith in Jesus, whom we cannot see with our eyes, and to open our hearts enough to see with the eyes of faith the miracles that are all around us.

My story begins a few weeks after my thirty-eighth birthday, in 2013, when I was admitted to the hospital for complications from pneumonia. I'd had trouble with my lungs for years, but when a pulmonary specialist found a large cavity in my lungs behind my heart, he was alarmed and sent me to Denver for further testing. After a week's worth of testing, the doctors thought I might have cystic fibrosis, a genetic lung disease, coupled with a life-threatening bacterial infection. I remember sitting in my hospital room with tears running down my face, saying, "This can't be happening. I have a five-year-old and an eight-year-old—they need their mom!" The more I read, the more the severity of my situation set in. The life expectancy for cystic fibrosis patients is thirty-eight—I was already living on borrowed time.

Reluctantly they let me go home to be with my family. A few weeks later, test results came back confirming the diagnosis of cystic fibrosis and a microbacterial infection that required heavy IV and oral antibiotics. Even with treatment, I had only about a 60 percent chance of beating the infection.

All I asked of my husband and a few close family members and friends, who had been praying for me, was that this be kept private. I did not want my two children to worry, and I didn't want to become a repeated topic of conversation in our small town. I wanted my family to live life as normally as possible.

Six months later, I had finished my daily IV antibiotics and tested negative for the bacteria. We were going to beat the infection! I continued on the oral antibiotics and just needed the tests to remain negative for one year. Then, just before the one-year mark, we received still more devastating news: tests revealed I had a new strain of microbacteria even stronger than the last; doctors gave me a 30 percent chance of beating it. This meant starting over with more IV antibiotics, plus inhaled and oral antibiotics as well. All this medication was taking its toll. My body was tired, and my confidence wavering.

Over lunch one day, a good friend who knew about the battle I was facing told me about a Catholic priest from Rwanda that led healing Masses at our local church. She offered beautiful examples of personal friends who had been healed at his prayer services. Even so, I was skeptical. *Likely just a coincidence*, I thought. At that time I was a lukewarm Christian at best, and at times I found myself doubting whether God was real.

And so a few months later in the fall of 2014, I was way out of my comfort zone when I found myself in the confessional in Our Lady of the Mountains Catholic Church, sitting directly in front of Fr. Ubald. At first being there felt overwhelming, yet I was also strongly convinced that this was exactly where I needed to be.

After Mass, Fr. Ubald put his hand on my head and prayed over me. He talked with me about the steps of forgiveness and healing. And then this man whom I had never met before in my life told me that he would pray for my healing every single day until he heard back from me. I will cherish that conversation as long as I live.

After hearing Fr. Ubald preach, I left Mass feeling strongly that I needed to forgive a friend and end an unnecessary feud between us. I also started going to Bible studies and began growing in my faith. A short time later, I received a phone call that my father had been hospitalized, and I was able to spend his last moments on earth holding his hand and talking with him. I'm convinced God made this possible so that we could have a chance to say what needed to be said, and my father could die in peace. All these things helped me to prepare for the healing God wanted to do in me.

Just after Christmas, I received an email from my doctor with the results of my latest tests. *The infection was gone.* On December 29, 2015, I sent this email to Fr. Ubald: "Thirty percent odds mean nothing when you have Jesus in your heart. I am in a better place, a stronger Christian. . . . I am forever grateful to you for doing God's work, making a difference in so many lives. Thank you for bringing me closer to our Lord and Savior. I will continue to share my testimony [in the] hope of making a difference for someone else."

Recently I watched Fr. Ubald's documentary *Forgiveness: The Secret of Peace*, and I was struck by his comment: "We may have lost the battle, but we will win the war." So many people today are fighting battles that others know nothing about. Fear and sin are everywhere, but God has given us weapons we need to fight the battle against evil. By his power, despite all odds, Jesus helps us to win the war. At times we may be wounded in the battle. But I have learned that if we offer our wounds to Jesus, he can heal us—physically, spiritually, and in every other way.

GOD HEALED MY EAR (LOS ANGELES—FEBRUARY 28, 2018)
As told by Rose Sweet

I adore you, O Lord. I breathed in the sweet, heady incense and my heart kept chanting quietly as Fr. Ubald raised Jesus in the monstrance. Then he turned to the people as he and Jesus came down into our midst. Processing through the softly singing crowd, he soon passed right in front of me.

O Jesus, I breathed. My heart was filled with such longing. I thought of the unnamed woman in scripture who touched the hem of Jesus' cloak (see Matthew 9:19–21). I reached out for the hem of Fr. Ubald's cope and quickly and discretely kissed it. He continued on, and I kept praying.

Later, at the ambo, Fr. Ubald shared that the Lord was revealing to him who had been healed. As I listened to these miraculous healings—crippled people getting up out of their wheelchairs, the deaf suddenly hearing, people with cancer claiming their cure—I knew these were not for me. I had always been in very good health and felt that the most important healing I could receive would be spiritual healing of my sinful heart.

But then Fr. Ubald said, "Someone here has had a healing of a sore just inside the ear."

Wait. What? Wait a minute! I'd had a nagging, painful, raw sore inside my right ear that would never heal. No ointment or medicine could fix it, and I'd lived with it for years. *Is the Lord really interested in healing such an insignificant problem?*

I reached inside my ear. The sore was gone. *Gone!* Inside I heard a voice say to me, "Yes, I know all about your sinful heart. But, Rosie, I am interested in all of you. Receive this small gift, and let it remind you that none of your struggles is too small for me. Remember that what I do in the body, I will also do in your heart."

JESUS HAS VISITED OUR FAMILY (JACKSON HOLE, WYOMING—2011 TO 2017)

As told by Cora Ligori

My husband, Jim, and I met volunteering at a summer camp in 2004. I was drawn to Jim because he loved kids and was very natural with them. I imagined him with his own children, and I knew he would be an amazing dad. We were married in the Holy Trinity Greek Orthodox Cathedral in Charlotte, North Carolina, on July 21, 2007; not long after this, we moved to Jackson, Wyoming. It was hard being so far from friends and family, and we were both starting new jobs.

We had discussed children and knew we wanted at least three. But I wanted to wait at least a year. When the time finally came and I was ready to start our family in January 2009, we were surprised to find that I didn't immediately become pregnant after coming off birth control. I was a healthy twenty-six-year-old woman, yet I was already showing signs of infertility, and the doctors couldn't explain why. We started infertility treatments, to no avail. I became discouraged.

In July 2010, my friend Katsey Long showed up at my work with Fr. Ubald, who had never had a teeth cleaning and who spoke very little English. As they left, Katsey invited everyone at the dental office to the healing service at the Catholic church that evening. Since I wasn't Catholic, I wasn't sure if I should go, but I ended up at the service with my sister, my best friend, and another coworker—each of us from a different church but all sisters in Christ. We sat at the back to see what would happen.

Through a French translator, Fr. Ubald began talking about a woman who wanted more than anything to become a mother, but the doctors couldn't explain why she hadn't conceived. "Treatments have failed, and she is discouraged," he continued. I began to cry, knowing that Jesus was speaking to me through him.

"Jesus says that you will become pregnant and will have several children. Just have hope and faith and be patient," Fr. Ubald continued. I went forward to claim the blessing, and he recognized me from the dental office. "My friend!" he said in English, and began to pray over me. I told Jim what had happened, and we decided to discontinue the infertility treatments and wait for God's timing.

In January 2011 I found out I was pregnant, but my joy quickly turned to sorrow when I began to bleed and we lost the baby. The doctor confirmed that I had miscarried the child we had wanted for so long.

In the spring of 2011, Fr. Ubald returned to Jackson and asked Katsey about me. Was I pregnant? Katsey had known about my miscarriage and told him what had happened. He asked to see me privately, and so I was invited to Katsey's home, where Fr. Ubald and I spent hours together talking and praying. He told me that he saw children around me, praying with us.

In October, Fr. Ubald visited Jackson again. I still wasn't pregnant, but we hadn't lost faith. River Crossing Church in Jackson hosted a Sunday evening service with Fr. Ubald, and I encouraged Jim to attend with me. When he invited those in need of healing to come forward for prayer, Jim and I went up together and held each other, praying to Jesus to heal me and to answer our prayers for children. Again I stood before the congregation and claimed my healing to come. Exactly two weeks later, I was pregnant.

At the end of July 2012 I ran into Fr. Ubald and Katsey at Grand Teton National Park. I was thirty-eight weeks pregnant with my daughter. Joyfully we greeted one another and celebrated God's answer to prayer. Elsie Sophia was born August 12.

The following March, Fr. Ubald returned to Jackson. The first thing he said after stepping off the plane was, "When do I meet my baby?" We brought Elsie to Katsey's home, and Fr. Ubald blessed her and prayed thanksgivings for God's faithfulness. Jim said to Fr. Ubald, "Elsie is evidence that Jesus has visited our family."

Years went by. You would think we would have learned, but we began infertility treatments again, this time a short course. Then Fr. Ubald returned to Jackson and reminded us that God had promised *multiple* children, not just one. So we discontinued the treatments . . . and in the fall of 2015, we told Fr. Ubald that another baby was on the way. The summer Elsie turned four, we welcomed George Anthony. Our cup had overflowed. Then, when George was just seven months old, I became pregnant again!

After George's birth, the doctors had asked us what we wanted to do about birth control. We just laughed and said we would take our chances. When I returned to the doctor early in my third pregnancy, we all had a good laugh! That November, James (Jamie) Dominic was born. Fr. Ubald got to hold him the next day, just before he returned to Rwanda. Together we recited the prayer of the psalmist:

> For You formed my inward parts;
> You covered me in my mother's womb.
> I will praise You, for I am fearfully *and* wonderfully made.
> Marvelous are Your works,
> And *that* my soul knows very well. . . .
> Your eyes saw my substance, being yet unformed.
> And in Your book they all were written,
> The days fashioned for me,
> When *as yet there were* none of them.
> (Ps 139:13–14, 16 NKJV)

FROM SUFFERING TO HEALING

Does it surprise you that Jesus continues to heal people today through his eucharistic presence? In the Gospel of Mark, Jesus said to his disciples, "These signs will accompany those who believe: in my name they will drive out demons, they will speak new languages. They will pick up serpents [with their hands], and if they drink any deadly thing, it will not harm them. *They will lay hands on the sick, and they will recover*" (Mk 16:17–18; emphasis added).

When Jesus said this to them, he made healing as a sign of his presence, a work of evangelization. We see Jesus working through the gift of healing, which he gave to his disciples, in Acts 3:1–10. There we see Peter and John going to pray in the Temple. Because they had agreed with what Jesus said, they prayed for sick people with faith. Peter said to a crippled beggar, "I have neither silver nor gold, but what I do have I give you: in the name of Jesus Christ the Nazorean, [rise and] walk" (Acts 3:6). And immediately the man stood up and walked.

The healing ministry is a way of evangelization, of leading people to encounter Jesus. It's one thing to speak about Jesus, but when I pray and Jesus heals, people realize that Jesus is in their midst. And then they realize that what he said is true: "I am with you always, until the end of the age" (Mt 28:20).

With healing ministry, when Jesus in his eucharistic presence brings healing to those present, either in the healing service or in eucharistic adoration, people realize that he is truly present. Many conversions have taken place because of this. People become more connected to Jesus by sincere prayer, for they believe he hears them because of the healings. They have prayed, and Jesus has answered—so they have faith that he hears prayers. The healings are the fruit of this prayer. What they have asked Jesus to do, he has done.

If Jesus is always present in the Eucharist, why doesn't everyone experience physical healing? When we open our hearts and invite Jesus to heal us, he knows best what kind of healing we need. Especially after the genocide, the healing people needed most was not always physical; sometimes it was emotional or spiritual. People's hearts needed to be healed and their ability to trust restored. Such healings are just as important as physical healings.

When Jesus brings healing to someone, the gift is intended not just for the one who is healed but also for all those who are present and all those who hear of the healing. When you see someone healed physically, your faith is strengthened. This is a healing as well—to realize that Jesus is alive. All who participate in these healing services receive what they need most from Jesus. They experience the touch of Jesus who is really alive.

I would invite you to come and attend a healing service if you are able to do so, so you, too, can experience the healing touch of Jesus. However, you do not have to attend a healing service to receive the healing touch of Jesus. If you have a need for healing, pray faithfully for Jesus to heal you. Ask your pastor or mature Christian friend to pray with you, asking Jesus to give you the healing you need.

If he does not give you physical healing right away, don't give up. Healing comes in many ways and always in God's time. If you are suffering, accept the pain with faith, knowing that every illness is an opportunity for healing. Sometimes Jesus heals us physically, and sometimes he strengthens us spiritually to endure suffering with trust and faith. Other times an illness leads to the ultimate healing, when we leave this life to experience perfect healing in the next.

I remember one time anointing a woman, and seeing her suffering, I cried. She touched me gently, "Don't worry, Father. I know Jesus is with me. I am ready to go and see him." She accepted her suffering willingly, and it consoled all who knew her. I believe it was Jesus who strengthened her to face death with confidence and trust.

It is difficult to watch the suffering of someone we know and love. And yet, if you pray for someone who is in pain, you are an instrument of Jesus. You are helping that person to carry their cross, as Jesus had Simon the Cyrene help him. You are helping that person to be healed as well—whether physically or interiorly.

Although it is true that we must be open to Jesus in order to receive healing, Jesus is not limited in whom he is able to heal. He will sometimes heal those who have not yet been converted as a sign of his reality. Other times the healing may be delayed until that person participates in his or her healing. I once knew a woman who had trouble swallowing; something was wrong with her throat and the doctor could not identify the source of the problem. She had been living with a man without being married and had stopped going to church because her conscience bothered her. Over time, she decided to leave this man and come back to church. She went to Confession and received the Eucharist. To her great surprise, when she received Jesus, she was able to swallow without any trouble. She was healed. She had encountered the healing Jesus in the Eucharist, and she praised God for it.

In healing people, Jesus gives us an opportunity to be witnesses for him. It is not good when people are healed and remain silent. We are healed to give witness to the presence of Jesus in the world. Those who are not healed physically, who accept their pain, also witness to Jesus in that acceptance in the name of Jesus.

Whether you are in need of physical healing or simply want to experience the presence of Jesus more fully in your life, Jesus is waiting for you.

Reflect

Do you have trouble believing that Jesus is truly present in the Eucharist or that he wants to heal you? When Jesus created the Eucharist, he said, "This is my body. This is my blood." This is when he created the Sacrament of the Eucharist, to fulfill his promise that he would never leave or forsake us. When we receive Communion, we receive the fruit of this presence—peace and healing.

At Mushaka parish, I knew a child who was born with an incurable wound on her jaw. She would go to the health center to get medicine, but nothing healed it. Then she received Jesus in First Communion when she was seven years old, and the next morning she came back to church to receive Communion again and go to adoration. She said to Jesus, "Jesus, I believe in you. I got you now. And you see I was born with this wound. Please heal it." The next day, the wound was healed. The fruit of the Eucharist was revealed in her life, and she went out and told all her friends about the Jesus who was alive in the Eucharist.

If you want to experience Jesus, go and spend time with him in the chapel, in eucharistic adoration. He is living and is ready to give you the healing you need—from depression, from doubt, or from whatever it is you need. He hears your prayer, and he wants to hear from you.

Do you continue to suffer from past experiences? Jesus understands what it is to be human, and what it is to suffer because of others. In the book of Hebrews we read, "Surely he did not help angels but rather the descendants of Abraham; therefore, he had to become like his brothers in every way, that he might be a merciful and faithful high priest before God to expiate the sins of the people. Because he himself was tested through what he suffered, he is able to help those who are being tested" (Heb 2:16–18).

Jesus knows how evil touches our lives and causes us to suffer. We cannot choose whether we will suffer; we can only choose how we will respond to the suffering. It can make us bitter or sweet, hard or gentle. How are you being tested? And how are you going to choose to respond?

In these stories, people bring their children and other loved ones to receive the healing they need. And yet family members can also inflict great suffering, inflicting wounds that are felt into adulthood. Have you suffered at the hands of a family member and even wish you had been born to a different family? Go back to Psalm 139 and read it again. What do you notice? What does it say to you about the healing power of God?

> For You formed my inward parts;
> You covered me in my mother's womb.
> I will praise You, for I am fearfully *and* wonderfully made.
> Marvelous are Your works,
> And *that* my soul knows very well. . . .
> Your eyes saw my substance, being yet unformed.
> And in Your book they all were written,
> The days fashioned for me,
> When *as yet there were* none of them.
> (Ps 139:13–14, 16 NKJV)

From the beginning, God chose your family—both biological and spiritual—who would help to shape the person you were to become. Sometimes they fail us, often because of their own wounds. We must forgive them and show them mercy, so that we can be free and at peace.

Forgiveness is also a way to share that freedom with others—including those who have hurt you. If you don't forgive, you remain spiritually closed. Renounce the abuse through forgiveness. Speak the truth so that your own family will not be burdened by the past. Even if the family member who hurt you never asks your forgiveness, you must continue to pray and show mercy.

Have you thanked God for each of your parents? Can you begin today?

In the fifth chapter of John, Jesus meets a man who had been lying beside a pool of water at Bethesda, where all the sick people of the community would go to be healed. This man had been unable to walk for thirty-eight years! Seeing him, Jesus asks him, "Do you want to be well?" (Jn 5:6).

Notice the man does not say yes right away. Instead, he blames others as the reason he has not yet received healing. So Jesus tells him to get up and walk, and he does.

Although it is Jesus who heals us, we must participate in our own healing. Don't blame others for not receiving the healing; it is not the fault of others. It is your responsibility, your opportunity, to receive healing. Even if others are praying for you, you must pray for yourself first. Others can help, but it is up to you.

Imagine Jesus standing before you, asking you the same question: "Do you want to be well?" How do you respond? What is keeping you from picking up your mat and running to claim that healing?

7.

A VISION OF THE FUTURE

Iyo mana dusenga irakomeye, dusenga irakomeye
(The God [to whom] we pray is powerful, he is powerful.)
Nimana itabura guseruka, Itabura guseruka.
(He never hides from us, he shows himself.)
—Rwandan gospel chorus

⊹)(⊹

"Muzungu! Muzungu!" Curious eyes turned toward my white Toyota Prado as high-pitched children's voices announced that white people were driving past. It was eight o'clock on a Tuesday morning, and yet the road leading up to the center was crowded with people, many of whom had been camped out since the previous evening. Some had come from the Congo, others from Kigali. It was a colorful crowd: men were dressed in Western-style suits, and women were in brightly colored national dress, balancing plastic tubs full of supplies on their heads or carrying large parasols, often with small children strapped to their backs. All of them had come on that thirteenth day of the month, as the Blessed Mother had requested at Fatima, to pray and turn their hearts toward God.

My editor and her husband had come to help me finish this final chapter of my book, and I was so happy that they were able to be here for this special event at the center, where

117

thousands and thousands of people had come together to pray and to find for themselves the secret of peace, which is forgiveness. I had someone seat them near an interpreter before going to the shelter to get ready. Already I could hear the choir, a hundred voices strong and dressed in snowy white robes, begin their praises.

> The King of Peace,
> Who owns all of earth and heaven,
> He is coming into our hearts. So be happy.
> He came to be with us. So be happy.

When it came time to preach, I reminded the people of Our Lady of Kibeho, who came to us in the decade prior to the genocide, weeping many tears because she had seen us killing one another. She was weeping because we would not listen. "But we are listening now, dear Mother. Do not weep anymore. Your children are listening to you now," I prayed.

I told the people of a man I had met recently while evangelizing at Kibeho. He had witnessed the killings there during the genocide and had become hardened against Christ and the Church. His wife, a devoted Catholic, had heard of a retreat I had arranged for the victims of genocide and urged him to go. At first he had refused. "Then as I was milking the cow," he said to me, "I decided I would go. So I called my wife to bring some water to wash with, and I went to the retreat."

When it came time to make a decision to forgive, the man rose to his feet and announced, "The first person I forgive is Jesus! He did not stop the killings. But I will forgive him." He sat down. A few days later, he was back again. "I have forgiven Jesus, and now I must beg pardon for myself."

"How many of you, like this man, have lost loved ones to violence and are finding it hard to forgive?" I asked those who were listening. "How many of you saw terrible things during the genocide, things that have robbed you of your peace? There is only one way to find peace. You must forgive.

"Close your eyes, and see Jesus standing in front of you. Go with him, in your mind, back to 1994. See those moments when your relatives were dying, being ushered into the arms of Jesus. Listen to them now—they are happy. 'What are you doing?' they say to you. 'See how happy we are now!'

"Let Jesus take your hand and lead you back. Listen as he speaks to the perpetrators. 'See those you killed? Do you see anger in their eyes? No—they are happier and more alive than they were before.' Can you see the difference between the love in their eyes, and the fear and anger you hold in your hearts?

"Now, look at the eyes of Jesus, you people who killed others. See the compassion he has for you, his son, his daughter. Even if you didn't kill but were happy to hear that others had died, Jesus has compassion for you as well. Go with him, and see all those people you thought had died. They are not dead. They are alive in heaven, with Jesus. And they have a message for you: 'We are the ones you killed, and we have a message you must take to the survivors. Jesus was there when we were killed, and he took us to heaven. If you will see that we are alive in Jesus and follow Jesus, you will be healed of your trauma. And you will be saved.'

"Jesus is here for you now, if you are ready to open the doors of your heart to him. First, you must have faith. Think of all that Jesus has done for you, from your childhood until now. Thank him for what he has done.

"Next, you must forgive those who have harmed you. And you must beg pardon and show mercy to those you have harmed. Do not seek revenge or deny your pain. Recognize that you have already been forgiven, and ask Jesus for the grace you need to walk in that forgiveness every day.[1]

"Resist evil. Look into your heart and see your deep-rooted sins. Ask Jesus to take them away, so that evil will not have a hold on you any longer.

"Decide today to live for Jesus, to live in God's love and to live a new life, starting today.

"Finally, accept the gift of peace he is offering you. Pray to be a friend of peace. Pray to be a witness to the love of God."

Later, after the Mass, I placed the Eucharist in the monstrance and began to process through the crowd, blessing the people with the eucharistic presence of Jesus. Some knelt silently with their heads bowed; others stood with arms upraised. The Holy Spirit was doing a powerful work. Six or seven people came up to witness to healings that had already taken place. One woman, holding an infant, gave praise to God for answering her prayers after seventeen years of infertility. "I had given up and had even stopped going to church because I was so angry with God for not giving me a child," she admitted. "But God did not forget me, and today I am here to beg pardon for all the times I did not trust God and stayed away from church because he did not give me what I asked for right away."

Others testified as well. One woman who had been plagued with severe headaches could now turn her head freely. Another who had anemia had been healed. A third with sciatica was able to walk without pain.

The service was nearly over when an American woman who was visiting stood up and gestured for an interpreter. "I want to thank God for allowing me to come here and to see this place. There is so much we can learn from what you have suffered. You think of America as a place of great wealth and opportunity—but there is also much spiritual darkness. Babies die by the thousands every day because their mothers refuse to give them life. Children die to gun violence. People are divided, hating and distrusting one another over cultural and political issues. Even those in the Church have experienced great pain. Please pray for us, your brothers and sisters in Christ, that we will learn from your experiences, that we would also learn the secret of peace. Thank you."

I later thanked her for her testimony. In Rwanda, many think that people in America have no struggles, no need for healing. This woman had given witness to the fact that the message of Our Lady is not only for Rwanda but also for people all over the world. So we must not be afraid to continue to tell the story of the genocide and of the power of God to bring healing even into the deepest divisions of every country in the world. Only as we continue to work together to bear witness to events of the past can we hope for a future of peace.

TRUTH AND UNITY: A VISION FOR RWANDA TODAY

On February 8, 2018, I attended the sixty-sixth annual National Prayer Breakfast in Washington, DC. It is here every year that leaders from around the world and across the United States pray together and build up relationships between nations.

This year's theme was forgiveness, and the opening prayer and keynote address at this event was offered by the

Fr. Ubald at the 2018 National Prayer Breakfast with Jeannette Kagame (center) and Immaculée Ilibagiza (right)

First Lady of Rwanda, Jeannette Kagame. Like St. Francis of
Assisi, she prayed that God would "bring love where there
is hatred. Bring pardon where there is offense. Bring truth
where there is error. Bring hope where there is despair."[2]

I thanked God to be able to witness this historic event
and to see Mrs. Kagame's powerful witness about the hard
lessons Rwanda has learned as we approach the twenty-fifth
anniversary of the genocide and to share those lessons with
the leaders of a country as powerful as the United States.
When light comes from America, because it is so powerful,
it spreads all over the world.

It is for many of these same reasons that I spend so
much of my time in America. When darkness comes from
America, it spreads all over the world—I like to think that if
light comes from America, that too will spread all over the
world. I was encouraged to hear several times at that breakfast people speak about forgiveness being necessary to stop
violence. Light is coming from America, and that is good.

The light of God has been slowly spreading in my homeland as well in the years since the genocide. Twenty-five years
later, Rwanda is once more flourishing, and I continue to
preach the message of forgiveness and mercy. The past is
never entirely forgotten, but there is a new sense of purpose
and unity. People are no more Tutsi or Hutu—we are all
Rwandan. My brother Révérien, who continues to serve in
the police of the Rwandan government, points to the Gacaca
courts and the national commitment to telling the truth of
what had happened as the reason we have come so far as a
country in a relatively short time:

> "The Gacaca courts were organized to help people rec-
> oncile and become productive members of society. This
> is how we managed to have a peaceful country in less
> than twenty years. There was so much to overcome—
> dead bodies, broken roads and buildings. We fought evil
> and conquered it, and now, twenty-five years later, we
> have the society we had dreamed of. We are all Rwan-
> dans now."

"There are still plenty of wounds. But unity and reconciliation is a choice. Our leadership made the roads and built a space for peace. Where there is injustice, the government stands up so the country cannot go back to the way it was. The leadership that is running the country is focused on building a peaceful and just society—and that makes it possible for Fr. Ubald to do what he is doing, without persecution or discrimination."

Twenty-five years after the darkness of the genocide, our people are making peace with themselves and with God. And within the Rwandan church, there are two places that I find to be especially bright lights of hope: the Missionaries of Peace and the Center for the Secret of Peace.

MISSIONARIES OF PEACE

The healing ministry that God had called me to undertake before the genocide became an important point of evangelization afterward. I had spent time in Europe in the months following the killings, resting and receiving the healing I needed at the Stations of the Cross at Lourdes. But when I returned to Rwanda and began to take up ministry again, the message I had preached before the genocide, about

The Missionaries of Peace of Christ the King

Sr. Donata Uwimanimpaye

giving and receiving mercy and forgiveness, was needed more than ever before.

So many people I met in the years following the genocide had left the Church, broken and disillusioned, and were unable to find their way back. I wanted to create a center where people could come to pray, and I envisioned creating a new order of religious brothers and sisters who could work for peace with me. To my surprise, as I continued to think and pray about this, I learned of Sr. Donata Uwimanimpaye, who had already begun to establish such a congregation. Sr. Donata belonged to the Benebikira Congregation, but after the genocide she had a vision for a new congregation that would work for peace.

The Missionaries of Peace of Christ the King began novitiate formation in 2009. The order now has about one hundred members throughout the country, including communities in the Cyangugu diocese, the Butare diocese, the Ruhengeri diocese, and the Kigali archdiocese. In Kibeho, where the Virgin Mary appeared starting in 1981, they are building the God the Father Chapel, recognizing that every human being has the same Father in heaven—a truth that had been lost in the genocide.

Bishop Thaddé Ntihinyurwa, who had ordained me, had tried to purchase land near Lake Kivu while he was bishop of Cyangugu to build a minor seminary there. But there were complications with the original purchase, and when the new bishop of Cyangugu, John Damascene, found out that I wanted to build the center on that property, he said, "If you want the land, help us to get the money to purchase it." All I needed was 200,000 euros (about 280,000 dollars).

I went to visit the property and heard a voice tell me, "This land belongs to you." And so, on my next trip to Europe, I began to share my vision for the Center for the Secret of Peace. And little by little, donations began trickling in. The woman who had helped pay my way through seminary gave me the first donation, worth two months of payments. Other friends from Germany, Austria, and America were equally generous, and within ten months, I had the entire amount. More money would be needed to build, but I was confident that Jesus had heard me and was providing for me.

When you listen to and follow Jesus, he always takes care of you.

Our work at the center is far from over, and we are trusting that God will provide what we need to build the church there as well as a convent for the Sisters of Peace and a home for elderly priests. We want to build a retreat house, a house for counseling, and other buildings needed for ministry. God alone knows where the money will come from. But God knows, and that is enough.

The church at the Center for the Secret of Peace, under construction as I write this, will seat one thousand people and will be used for perpetual adoration. People can come there to be close to Jesus and cover the center in prayer.

Coming Home: The Making of *Forgiveness: The Secret of Peace*

As I continued to travel to America and Europe to conduct healing services and to share my story, a generous benefactor offered to fund the cost of a documentary that would allow me to share the healing God had done after the genocide to a wider audience. In January 2015, we took our first film crew to Rwanda to begin filming *Forgiveness: The Secret of Peace*. We completed the editing process in July 2017.[3]

As I went back to my home village and the other places that had been so important to me, I was so thankful that I could see everything once more, this time with new eyes. As I approached my village, my heart was full of emotion. I remembered many good family memories of the times I spent with my mother and family. I felt so much joy then—not like in 1995, when there was so much darkness in my heart and everything was bad. Now I could smile and embrace my homeland with peace and joy.

I could tell that this newfound sense of peace and joy had settled all around. By this time everyone knew who had been involved in the killings and who had not. Now when I meet people who still live there, we are no longer afraid of one another. Most of those who needed to have begged pardon from the victims and are no longer afraid of us. Even those who are not open, who refuse to beg pardon, continue to come to us, hoping to build up new relations.

There are still times when mercy is needed so that seeds of peace may grow. When I was there for the documentary, I learned that one man who had killed my cousin was afraid to meet me face-to-face. Instead he said to another, "I want to meet Fr. Ubald because I have killed a member of his family." I assured the man who brought this message that I have forgiven the man who killed my cousin.

I understood the reason this man was afraid to come to me. In the years following the genocide as I went to preach in the prisons, I often encountered men who were afraid to face the families of those they had harmed. They were like sheep that had run away, destroying crops and causing trouble. They would not yet listen to the shepherd's voice. I had seen that a good shepherd must go and bring back the sheep, even if it meant a lot of trouble and even sometimes pain. This is what it means to be a good shepherd.

And this is the task God has appointed for me: I am like a shepherd to these sheep that have run away and are afraid to follow the shepherd's voice. Jesus said, "I have other sheep, that do not belong to this fold. These also I must lead, and they will hear my voice, and there will be one flock, one shepherd" (Jn 10:16). And so I continue to preach, and I continue to speak of mercy and forgiveness as the path to healing. I preach it here in Rwanda, and I preach it wherever the opportunity arises elsewhere. For there are other sheep, all over the world, who need to hear this message, that forgiveness is the secret of peace.

FROM CONFLICT TO PEACE

Over time, as we continue to walk in forgiveness and mercy, God will often grant new opportunities for growth and ministry, redeeming the pain of the past.

In the twenty-five years since the genocide, I have met countless men and women who because of Jesus found the courage to forgive what would have been impossible to forgive on their own power. In this final chapter, two such people, Jean Claude Ntambara and Claudette Mukarumanzi, share their story in order to help those who are struggling to resolve their inner conflicts in order to find peace.

At the time of the genocide, Jean Claude was a police officer in the Kanzenze Commune, near Bugesera. He recalled that during the early 1990s, he and his associates were being told that Tutsis were coming to kill them and that they must be prepared to resist. "They told us that the Tutsis were evil and that they needed to be stopped—but

we had no idea that they were referring to genocide," said
Jean Claude.

Then in March 1992, a "trial genocide" erupted in Bugesera. Tutsi homes were pillaged and burned, and people
were killed. "These were our neighbors," said Jean Claude.
"Although the militia did the actual killings, we had orders
not to protect the citizens or to try to stop the killings. I was
a young man at the time, without family. If I had intervened,
I would have received the same treatment. We brought as
many as we could to the local church with their belong-
ings. That time, at least, those who made it to the church
remained safe.

"In 1994, all that changed. When the president's plane
was shot down, we were ordered by government officials to
start killing Tutsis. These were our neighbors and friends,
who had never done anything wrong to us and who had
come to us for protection. But we had failed them. From
April 11 until May 12, when the RPF [Rwandan Patriotic
Front] took control of the area, I continued the killings. Then
we went to the Congo on foot and arrived there on July 17,
1994. After two years, the RPF destroyed the camps so we
would be forced to come back. But I was afraid to come
back. I stayed in the forest and continued a kind of guerilla
warfare, along with some others, until 1998, then returned
to the Congo. In 2001 I heard that the danger was past and
decided to return.

"I returned in 2001 and submitted to the traditional
justice system in Gando, similar to Gacaca courts. We were
brought back into society if we voluntarily pleaded guilty
for our crimes. I was sentenced to twenty years, but it was
reduced to fourteen years of community service, building
roads and buildings. I lost my job as a policeman.

"When I finished my sentence, Fr. Ubald invited a group
of us who had committed genocide to come to a retreat at
Nyamata parish. On the fourth day, they spoke to perpetrators, and I learned that I needed to ask forgiveness from
those I had harmed. On the fifth day, I met Claudette. We

were practically strangers—I had known about her when she was a little girl, but now she was a grown woman.

"And it was then, at that retreat, that I learned I had been the one who shot her—not just once but three times. And yet she had survived."

Claudette sat quietly as Jean Claude told his story, insisting that she would tell her story when he was finished. When it came time for her to speak, she reached up to her shoulder and revealed a deep scar where soldiers—*that* soldier—had shot or bludgeoned her on three separate occasions. She showed us another mark on her scalp, this one covered by her hair. And then she began her story.

"I was the fourteenth child in my family, and I'd had a very happy life in a family full of love. In 1992 I started losing members of my family: my brother and his wife and their seven children were killed in the trial genocide. We later learned that it had been our neighbors who had done this—they had fried the children in oil and cut off my brother's legs before closing him and his wife inside the burning house.

"There was an Italian woman, Antonia Locatelli, who tried to tell the world what was happening—she called people in Italy and told them. The Hutu killed her. Her grave is at the memorial at Nyamata.

"When at last we came out of hiding and learned what had happened, we went to Fidele Rwambuka, the burgomaster, to report them. But he refused to make a report. No one would acknowledge what had happened."

"We had been ordered just to let things be," cut in Jean Claude.

Claudette continued, "In 1993, peace seemed to come back because of the Arusha Accords. Then in 1994, after the plane crash, they started burning our houses, and everyone ran into the hills or to the churches for sanctuary. The police went up into the hills and started shooting, driving everyone back toward the churches. As the circle they made around us tightened more and more, I hid in the bushes with my big sister, a newlywed, and her husband and two children. Then when my sister and her family were killed, I escaped to the commune and then to the church. 'I will go to God's house,' I said to myself. 'God will know what to do.'

"Inside the church, people were dying of hunger. We had no food or water. Then on April 14, someone threw a gas grenade into the sanctuary to blind the victims and cause them to run out. The killers brought machetes, maces, axes, any tools that could kill. One man ran and hit my sister on the temple; then another man shot me through the shoulder. Jean Claude saw that it had not killed me and took another shot that destroyed my shoulder. I laid still, even when the killers came through later and began sexually assaulting our bodies to see who was still alive. I was careful not to flinch.

"Much later, different men came in and gathered up the Tutsis who were still alive and brought them to the priest's house [to try to help them]. But when they turned on the water taps, blood flowed out. Someone had filled the water tank with bodies.

"The next morning the killers came back—including Jean Claude, whom I had hoped would help me find my family. I told him who I had seen alive and where they had been hiding. Then he took a mace to my temple, and another speared me in the back. I fell into a pile of debris, which contaminated my wound. Somehow I managed to pull out the spear. Then I looked around for some food, but there was none. At that point people were eating little balls of clay. A few days later, intruders came back and brought a dead cow, forcing us to eat the meat raw. It was a way to torture us, to show they had power over [us] even when we died.

"One day I saw people being lined up and killed, including my sister and her husband. I met up with an old lady and child, and we ducked into a house. The perpetrators followed us, but I hid and they found only the other two. 'Tell us where she is, or we will throw you into the toilets.' And they did. I hid all night until the next morning.

"The next morning I ran to a pastor's house, and he hid me in the pigsty—then called the police to come and get me. And it was Jean Claude who came again. He struck me once more in the shoulder, the same place he had hit before and that had begun to fester. With that blow, it was as if my strength left me. They threw me into the toilet. Eventually they began throwing other bodies into the toilet as well, until I could finally climb up and get out.

"I wasn't stronger than anyone else. But if God says you are going to live, you will live. It doesn't matter if they take away your humanity; you will live. And God was with me."

How was it possible that Claudette was able to look at Jean Claude, who had inflicted so much pain on her and had tried to kill her several times and forgive him from her heart? Claudette says her "trip," her journey to reconciliation with Jean Claude is a holy story.

"After the genocide, when he had finished his sentence and I saw him in the village, I felt ill at the sight of him—I became nauseated and had terrible headaches. My whole body reacted to the trauma. Then one day Fr. Ubald gave his reconciliation talk, and Jean Claude came to me and to another woman whose parents he had killed. I knew it was the only way to find peace, and as I saw him on his knees, begging for our forgiveness, I told him that I forgave him. But I didn't mean it in my heart.

"I continued to avoid him and felt sick when I saw him. After a while Jean Claude realized something was wrong, so he came to my house. When I wasn't home, he left a message with his number. I never called, and he showed up at my house five or six times to talk to me. I left him outside and refused to let him in my house. He came so often that the tires on his bike were wearing thin.

"One day when he came to my house, his wife was with him. When I saw her, I knew I couldn't leave her outside—she had done nothing wrong. So I invited her inside and called the other woman whose parents he had killed. 'Come, and let's receive them,' I said to her.

"So he came in with his wife, and for the first time I was able to look at him in his eyes. This time I forgave him from my heart, and we sat eating and talking together. Up until then I had avoided going to church as well—too many bad memories. It was Jean Claude who brought me back to church. I figured, if he can go to church, why can't I?"

Jean Claude nodded. "I was not able to receive Communion at that time—I had to go through catechism and be formally received back into the Church. Claudette was my sponsor."

Claudette smiled. "My life is much better now. I don't get sick from the trauma anymore, and I've been able to finish my schooling. I have four children, although I am no longer with their father. Best of all, Jean Claude and his wife are like family to me. Together we solve our problems as family members do. And when we go to heaven, we will go there together. He is no longer a killer—he is my brother."

Jean Claude and Claudette

In the story of Claudette Mukarumanzi and Jean Claude Ntambara, we see that it can take time for conflicts to be resolved so that both sides can experience freedom. Forgiveness is not always something that happens instantly; it can take a long time of making daily choices to show mercy to the other person.

If while reading this book the Holy Spirit has been reminding you of unresolved conflicts and pain from the past, the time has come to claim the blessing of peace for yourself and your loved ones. Do not be afraid or try to cover the truth of what has happened. Jesus already knows it all. If you need assistance, speak to a priest or other mature Christian who can pray with you and support you as you find ways to show forgiveness and mercy to those who have harmed you, so that you may be free of your burden and be truly free. God bless you.

Reflect

Is it difficult for you to imagine God's purpose for allowing you to suffer or to trust him for your future? Listen to what God's Word says to you: "For I know well the plans I have in mind for you . . . plans for your welfare and not for woe, so as to give you a future of hope. When you call me, and come and pray to me, I will listen to you. When you look for me, you will find me. Yes, when you seek me with all your heart" (Jer 29:11–13).

Don't worry about the future. Jesus is next to you. He has always been with you, and he will always be with you. Try to stay connected to him.

The one who receives the light of Jesus and is converted must continue to be a witness in the world, so that others might find this same peace. This is what Jesus says to us:

> You are the salt of the earth. But if the salt loses its taste, with what can it be seasoned? It is no longer good for anything but to be thrown out and trampled underfoot. You are the light of the world. A city set on a mountain

cannot be hidden. Nor do they light a lamp and then put it under a bushel basked; it is set on a lampstand, where it gives light to all in the house. Just so, your light must shine before others, that they may see your good deeds and glorify your heavenly Father. (Mt 5:13–16)

When bad things happen, Jesus can use even these things—such as the genocide—to give a message to the world. Right now a light is coming from Rwanda and spreading all over the world as people come from all over to learn how Rwandans are making efforts to live together in peace again after living through such horror.

Are you ready to give this light and salt to others, by forgiving and begging pardon, even from bad things? Jesus can help you to do this, when you ask him to help. Are you ready to be the one whom Jesus can use to transform the world?

After the Resurrection, Jesus appeared to his disciples to encourage them and to guide them to continue the work he had entrusted to them. Appearing suddenly in the Upper Room, he said these words to them: "Peace I leave with you; my peace I give to you. Not as the world gives do I give it to you. Do not let your hearts be troubled or afraid" (Jn 14:27).

Jesus said, "Peace I give you." The disciples had been staying behind closed doors; they had forgotten that Jesus had already given them the peace they needed, peace that is not available in the world. Jesus appears to remind them of this gift, a gift that no one and nothing can take away from them.

Refusing to forgive will steal your peace. Seeking revenge will rob you of your peace. Refusing to beg pardon to one you have wronged will take away your peace. Resist these temptations. They are from the evil one. Jesus has given peace to all believers; no one can take it away from you. Whatever has happened, stay close to Jesus and you will find peace. Turn your face toward Jesus, and refuse to give in to temptation. Entrust your troubles to God, and you will find peace again.

In his final moments on earth, Jesus spoke to his disciples to say his final words to them on the mountain of Galilee, commissioning them to spread the Gospel to the end of the earth: "All power in heaven and on earth has been given to me. Go, therefore, and make disciples of all nations, baptizing them in the name of the Father, and the Son, and of the holy Spirit, teaching them to observe all that I have commanded you. And behold, I am with you always, until the end of the age" (Mt 28:18–20).

To proclaim the Good News is a task of all Christians. In Rwanda, we had lost this message and had nothing to proclaim because of the evil fruit of genocide; the Gospel in Rwanda would have been lost unless we changed. But as we acknowledged the darkness in which we were living and accepted change, we were able to proclaim the message once more, becoming preachers and witnesses of reconciliation and forgiveness.

Those who preached and those who had received the message before the genocide both needed to be reconverted. Only then would we be able to continue to be messengers of peace and love. Jesus had not failed us; we needed to turn our hearts back to him so we could beg pardon and receive healing.

Do you also want to be involved in this great work of evangelization? Do you want to be a witness to what God has done for you, to bring change where it is most needed? Bad things come from evil; do you accept that we must fight this evil and resist it with the power of the Holy Spirit? The best days are before us. Trust in Jesus.

8.

PRAY WITH FR. UBALD

A Guided Meditation

For you say, "I am rich and affluent and have no
need of anything," and yet do not realize that you
are wretched, pitiable, poor, blind, and naked. . . .
 Those whom I love, I reprove and chastise. Be
earnest, therefore, and repent. "Behold I stand at the
door and knock. If anyone hears my voice and opens
the door, [then] I will enter his house and dine with
him, and he with me."
—Revelation 3:17, 19–20

I have traveled all across the world. I have seen many souls
encounter the healing touch of Christ in the Eucharist, and
I have witnessed people receive spiritual and even physical
healing by opening their hearts to Christ. And so, in this
closing chapter, I would like to share with you a prayer
exercise that will help you to open your heart to the Lord
and invite the Holy Spirit to begin a new work in your heart.
 God alone can give us the strength to break the bonds
of distrust and disunity between people, within parishes or
communities, and among nations. In every case, we experience this strength that brings freedom through five spiritual
keys.

THE FIVE SPIRITUAL KEYS: A PRAYER EXERCISE

Find a quiet place to sit and pray without distraction—perhaps a chapel where eucharistic adoration is offered. Bring your Bible and a notebook, if you wish. As you work through each exercise, concentrate on sitting with Jesus and listening to his voice. You don't need to do the whole exercise at once. Just come back each time and put yourself in the Lord's presence and ask him to speak to you and to bring healing where you need it most.

Key 1: Faith

As you sit with Jesus, ask yourself if there is any place in your heart that is off limits to the Lord, that feels hard or closed off. Are you willing to open your heart to him so he can enter?

To open our hearts to Jesus, we must first use the key of *faith*. As you look back on your life, have you ever said something such as, "God has abandoned me"; "Where are you, God?"; or, "I don't see God at work in my life"? But in the Gospel of Matthew, Jesus said, "And behold, I am with you always, until the end of the age" (28:20).

Ask Jesus to show you where God has done things for you, from your childhood until now. Make a trip in your heart to see how God has been so good to you. He has done so many good deeds and has been so merciful even from your childhood. This is the key of faith. Acknowledge the many times that God took good care of you. Then, as you are thinking about it, thank him and be grateful.

If you wish, record in your journal or notebook the thoughts and impressions that came to you after you asked the Lord to reveal where he has been at work in your life.

Key 2: Forgiveness

Because God has been so good to you, when he asks you to do something, don't refuse him. God, who has been so good, asks us to forgive. And so we choose to forgive—and to ask for forgiveness from those we have harmed—because God has been good to us and we know we can trust his goodness.

Imagine yourself holding a key that will unlock the chains that are binding this person to you, so you can cast aside this heavy burden. Go back over your life and try to remember everyone who has done wrong to you, from your childhood to now. Perhaps your parents, brothers or sisters, neighbors, teachers, or others have wounded you in a significant way. Think of all those who have hurt you, and make a decision to forgive. Forgive without any condition, as a free gift.

How often must we forgive? Peter asks this same question in the Gospel of Matthew: "Lord, if my brother sins against me, how often must I forgive him? As many as seven times?" Jesus answered, "I say to you, not seven times but seventy-seven times" (Mt 18:21–22). This doesn't mean the other person has a "right" to be forgiven. Forgiveness is a gift. What the other person has done to you may seem unforgiveable on a human level, such as genocide. But still we must forgive. We learn this from Jesus, who said from the Cross, "Father, forgive them, they know not what they do" (Lk 23:34). He gave the example of forgiveness without condition.

Sometimes we say, "Oh, I want to forgive, but he doesn't want pardon." Forgive anyway. Open the door of forgiveness from your side, so you can be free. Very often, showing mercy to those who have wronged us will give them the courage to receive the gift and open the door from the other side. If you show mercy, they will know it is safe to ask your forgiveness. Without mercy, they will never trust in your forgiveness.

Genuine forgiveness—or genuine contrition or regret—is always expressed with mercy. If the person who has harmed you or whom you have harmed has died, extend that mercy by praying for him or her, or by showing mercy to his or her family. Without mercy, forgiveness is incomplete.

If you do not show mercy, the darkness in your heart will begin to grow again and extinguish the light of forgiveness.

The key of forgiveness is also needed if you have been bad to someone else. Ask God to reveal to you those you have harmed and from whom you need to beg pardon. Don't make excuses or justify your actions. Instead, consider how you can show mercy and compassion toward those you have wronged. When one who forgives is merciful and one who begs pardon receives mercy, reconciliation is possible. If we want to change society, we must begin by being merciful to one another.

If you wish, record in your journal or notebook the names of the people you have thought of whom you need to seek forgiveness from or need to receive forgiveness from you. Ask the Lord to show you where to begin.

Key 3: Deliverance

There are several kinds of evil spirits stirring up trouble in the world. If there is a particular sin, such as anger, pride, or lust, that you bring to Confession repeatedly, you may need to renounce its hold on your life in the name of Jesus.

Do you have trouble with anger, pride, envy, or unforgiveness? Do certain sins continue to make problems in your family, such as drugs, sexual habits, envy, or anger? Renounce and resist them in the name and by the authority of Jesus. "You belong to God, children, and you have conquered them, for the one who is in you is greater than the one who is in the world" (1 Jn 4:4).

Ask Jesus to show you if there are any spiritual influences he wants to break in your life. Write down the sinful habits that keep you away from God or create difficulties in your family, and ask God to remove them from your life in the name of Jesus.

Key 4: Deciding to Live for Christ

After allowing God to work in your life through forgiving, receiving pardon, and renouncing evil, you are ready to make a decision to live for Christ. If you have already been baptized, you will cooperate with those sacramental graces in a new, more intentional way. If you have not yet been baptized, go to church and ask how you can begin preparing to be baptized. All of the sacraments, including Eucharist and Confession, strengthen us to become disciples of Jesus and to follow him faithfully each day.

You must decide that you want to please God in everything and renounce those things you know displease him. As you seek to be in good relationship with God, living in obedience to the Holy Spirit, you will learn to be like him and find it easier living in union with other people.

Begin everything you do by asking if it will be pleasing to Jesus. If not, don't do it. Decide that you will only do things that keep you in close connection with Jesus. Once you have made this decision, you must begin to act on it right away, for "now is the day of salvation" (2 Cor 6:2b).

Have you decided to start a new life in Christ today? Record this decision in your journal. Ask Jesus to help you identify what is pleasing and displeasing to him. What changes do you need to make, starting today?

Key 5: Receiving God's Blessings

Ask God to bless you and your life. Jesus will send his blessing and mercy upon you: "All good giving and every perfect gift is from above, coming down from the Father of lights, with whom there is no alteration or shadow caused by change" (Jas 1:17).

There are many ways to get close to God in order to receive the blessings he wants to give to you. Spend time in prayer, reading the Word of God. Visit with Jesus at your parish or in a nearby adoration chapel. Receive the sacraments often, especially the Eucharist and Reconciliation (Confession). Ask Jesus to heal you, body and spirit. There are many spiritual and physical healings that can take place when you make this trip in your heart and begin to make a new life as a friend of Jesus.

As you complete this exercise, write a prayer to Jesus, thanking him for the many blessings he has given you and for his love and protection in your life. Ask him to show you if there is a particular area of your life that needs healing, and ask him for his blessing in your life. Return as often as you can to spend time in his presence, allowing him to continue this healing work in your heart.

ACKNOWLEDGMENTS

There are so many people I need to thank who contributed to my being able to share my story here. Above all, I want to thank God the Father; his Son, Jesus; and the Holy Spirit, for bringing each of these people into my life, so that these dreams—the book, the documentary, and the Center for the Secret of Peace in Rusizi, Rwanda—might become realities.

I want to thank my family, especially my mother, Anysie Mukaruhamya. I was seven years old and the eldest of four children when she became a widow in 1963 at the age of thirty-two. I am so grateful for her and for her affection. Many times she said to us, "I don't want to listen to people saying that you just failed in life because you did not have a father's presence." She built strong character in her children; she was a mother as well as a father to me. She did not hate those who made her a widow, and I learned from her how to forgive. She was killed during the genocide in Rwanda in 1994. May she rest in peace.

Archbishop Thaddé Ntihinyurwa was bishop of the Cyangugu diocese when he ordained me to the priesthood in 1984. He allowed me to realize my life's dream: to preach God's love as a priest in Rwanda. During the genocide in Rwanda, he protected me by bringing me to his house, and after the genocide he allowed me to stay in the Kigali archdiocese where he was archbishop. There I began the work of evangelization, preaching about forgiveness and reconciliation and praying for healing, specifically for inner wounds. I thank God for him.

In the years since the genocide, God has called me to work for peace and reconciliation in my homeland. I could not have accomplished this work on my own; many people have helped me, both in Rwanda and in the United States.

I am so grateful to Paul Kagame, president of Rwanda, who had the courage to save our country, which had been devastated by turmoil between ethnic groups. Because of his vision for our country, today every Rwandan is now proud to be Rwandan, and because of his determination, he pursues good things for his people. I have learned so much from him. Blessings to him and to his family. I am also grateful to his wife, First Lady Jeanette Kagame; through her engagement in peacemaking, she is truly a mother to our country.

When I began to preach and work for forgiveness and reconciliation at Mushaka parish, many people were against me and distrusted me, saying that my initiatives would divide Rwandans. They were afraid to listen to me preach forgiveness and reconciliation because of their inner wounds. But at a speech on the fiftieth anniversary of the foundation of Mushaka parish, First Lady Jeanette Kagame congratulated me for helping Rwandans not only by preaching about forgiveness but also by encouraging the perpetrators of genocide against the Tutsi to beg pardon. She saved me from those who were preparing discrimination against me. Her speech encouraged me to go ahead preaching about forgiveness and reconciliation not only in Rwanda but also all over the world. Blessings to her.

I also want to remember some others who helped me during my seminary years. Traude Schröttner was a member of Karlau parish in Austria, which paid for my theological studies when I was in major seminary. Traude visited me for the first time in 1988, when I was pastor at Nyamasheke parish, and she visited my mother during that time as well. After the genocide I went for a rest in Graz, Austria, where she was living. I was grieving the loss of my mother and other family members, and she said to me, "I will be your mother to you now." During that time, I lived with Fr. Karl Thaller, pastor of Karlau parish; he was a holy man who passed away on May 27, 2018, just two weeks after the last

As a father, Denny had great spiritual influence on all his children, who have also actively supported the work of God. Caroline Long, his daughter, created the St. Gerard House, a school for autistic children in North Carolina. Two of his other children have also been a tremendous help to me in my own ministry. Patrick Long was a filmmaker and the executive director and a producer of *Forgiveness*, though he passed away in July 2016, before the final edit was completed. May he rest in peace.

Katsey Long, the executive producer and director of the film, organizes my evangelization schedule whenever I come to the United States and has welcomed me so often since my first visit in 2009 to Jackson Hole, Wyoming, it has become like my second home, thanks to the many friends I've made there. Katsey is a psychologist and sociologist who uses Christian listening techniques to help people struggling with inner wounds and depression. I met her the very first time I came to America in 2009. I was with Fr. Lescheck Czelusniak, with the Marian Fathers of the Immaculate Conception who serve at the Cana Center in Kibeho-Nyarushishi in Rwanda. He was known by the pastor of the Our Lady of the Mountains parish in Jackson Hole, and I was invited to say Mass and offer healing prayers there. Jesus healed many people, including a young woman named Carmen, who is now free from leukemia. Some time later, Katsey visited me in Rwanda and brought two companions, Paul Vogelheim and Denis Dolff. When they arrived at the area that was to become the Center for the Secret of Peace, they exclaimed, "This place near the lake gives peace; the dream must become reality!" Paul is a dynamic member of Rotary International at Jackson Hole, and he engaged the members of Rotary International to sustain the Center for the Secret of Peace by building toilets and providing water at the center. Paul Vogelheim is my brother, and I am so grateful for what he did for the center.

Since 2009, Katsey has organized many evangelization services for me in America and introduced me to people interested in helping sustain projects at the center. She loves Rwanda, and she has visited it many times and does all that she can to help Rwanda heal from the wounds of genocide. She has been involved in peacemaking for Rwanda, and in addition to helping me make the documentary, she was instrumental in helping me to write this book. Without her, this book would not have been created. Many thanks to her and blessings.

I met Sophie Craighead for the first time in 2010 while staying at Jackson Hole with Katsey, and I shared with her my dream of creating the Center for the Secret of Peace. She took interest in the project and has supported the center many times, including when we worked on terraces, spiritual streets, and the church. Every time I met her she was eager to know how the building of the center was progressing. She has provided much support to the Center for the Secret of Peace. Sophie brings joy wherever she is, and she has encouraged me many times by telling me that the center is a work of Jesus that Jesus himself will work on. Thank you so much, Sophie, for your support the Center for the Secret of Peace. You are really a peacemaker.

Gregory Thrompson visited Rwanda in August 2017. He prayed as he climbed the steps to the Merciful Jesus statue at the Center for the Secret of Peace. I was considering building a church at the center, and he encouraged me to start building with only a little money. He said this project belonged to Jesus, not to me. And with his words, my fear of beginning the project disappeared. I am thankful for him and for his prayers that the church would be finished so that people could adore Jesus in the Sacrament of the Eucharist.

I met Dr. Mary Tamara for the first time in Green Bay, Wisconsin. She joined the congregation at the National Shrine of Our Lady of Good Help and was healed of a disease similar to epilepsy, which made her fall down frequently. Today she cures clients and speaks to them of Jesus—she says that while she cures them, Jesus heals them. She and her husband converted to the Catholic faith when she experienced Jesus alive in the Eucharist. I praise God for her work and her faithful witness.

I also want to thank Bill Hayes, whom I met at the prayer breakfast in Washington, DC, in February 2018. He took interest in the Center for the Secret of Peace. He wants to work for peace in the world with me. I welcome him as I welcome you who read this book. Let us work for peace; when people love each other then there is peace, and there is no peace without love.

Finally, I would like to thank some others who encouraged me to put my story in book form. Dr. Mary Neal is an orthopedic surgeon and author of the book *To Heaven and Back*. After reading that book, which touched my heart and spirit, I asked her how she had time to write a book. She answered me, smiling, that the secret to writing a book is determination. She told me how, when awake at three in the morning, she sat down and began to write. She encouraged me to write a book and share my experience of forgiveness and reconciliation to the world, saying that the message I was giving was not only for Rwanda and Catholics; it was universal. I am so grateful to her because the idea to write a book flourished inside me after I met her.

Heidi Hess Saxton worked with me in writing this book. I met her for the first time in a conference organized by WINE: Women In the New Evangelization. Meeting her was a grace. She introduced herself to me as an editor, and I asked her if she could work with me. She immediately agreed and began to work with me. Her rhythm of work obliged me to work hard also, and I finished writing in time so that this book can help people in Rwanda commemorating the twenty-fifth anniversary of genocide. The message given in the book is universal: If the Rwandan people can forgive and beg pardon after genocide, who can't forgive or seek forgiveness after conflict?

I met Monique Stevens for the first time at the shrine to Our Lady of Good Help in Green Bay, Wisconsin. She was healed from a sun allergy and has since brought many other people to receive healing in her home near Chicago, Illinois. She has also opened her home to me so that I could have a quiet place to write this book.

There are so many others I could name who have been a blessing to me, so many parishes that have invited me to pray with them, and so many people who have given witness to the healing love of Jesus. In Rwanda, I have been blessed by the people of Ntendezi, Nyamata, Rugango, Simbi, Kibirizi, and Kibungo parishes. In the United States, there have been so many more. God bless you all!

The work of reconciliation in Rwanda continues, as people continue to seek peace within themselves and among one another. I am grateful to parishioners of Mushaka parish, that they were open to the Holy Spirit and willing to receive the help they needed to be healed of inner wounds from the genocide. Their experience of forgiveness and reconciliation has become a light to the world. It also helped me to heal from my own sense of failure after many of my parishioners were caught up in the genocide. Thank you so much to Mushaka parishioners.

I am so grateful to Fr. Eric Nzamwita who succeeded me at Mushaka parish and didn't give up in the pastoral role of encouraging parishioners to continue the work of forgiveness and reconciliation. He supported and accompanied Mushaka parishioners to go and share their experience of forgiveness and reconciliation throughout Rwanda. The light from Mushaka parish is now spreading all over the world. People are coming now from all over the world to witness how people forgave and begged pardon after genocide. Evil spirits of division continue to attack us from outside, trying to discourage the work. Yet Fr. Eric Nzamwita has persevered; the initiative I began at Mushaka parish continues today because of him. Thanks be to God!

APPENDIX

About the Mushaka Reconciliation Project

This is an abridged version of the "Mushaka Parish Reconciliation Project: Forgiveness as a Way to Rebuild the Bridge of Good Relationships between Rwandese People." This document was developed in December 2014 by Fr. Ubald, J. E. Nzamwita, and other community leaders to map out a peacemaking process that could be used in other parishes seeking to facilitate reconciliation after the genocide. More information about this process is available online on Fr. Ubald's website, https://frubald.com, and may be used by groups who want to facilitate peacemaking in their own parishes.

INTRODUCTION: THE PROCESS OF UNITY AND RECONCILIATION
THAT MUSHAKA PARISH HAS UNDERTAKEN

Twenty years after the genocide against the Tutsis, which took the lives of 1,074,017[1] innocent people, Rwandans from all sides looked for ways to bring about self-reconstruction and rehabilitation. The ongoing challenges were clear: it was impossible to ensure the safety and security of either ethnic group until both sides were prepared to set aside differences and work together for unity and lasting peace. Those who had been charged with violent crimes and had served their sentences that had been legally imposed upon them needed to experience an ongoing desire for reconciliation and peace. Both sides needed to acknowledge and address the underlying injustices, real and perceived, that had given rise to systematic violence. For both sides, forgiveness was needed to bring about healing on both a personal and national level.

The Church has both an opportunity and a moral imperative to facilitate this process of reconciliation and to end the ongoing conflict and unrest. Survivors and perpetrators of the violence alike continue to gather each Sunday in churches, each fearful of the violence that continues to threaten. Until the underlying conflict is resolved, authentic reconciliation is prevented as ongoing patterns of lying, self-justification, and avoidance continue to frustrate the effort to work together for peace and genuine unity.

Church leaders, especially priests and clergy, must be willing to lead by example this process of reconciliation within their own parishes. "But all is of God, who has reconciled us to himself through Christ, and who has given us the ministry of reconciliation. For certainly God was in Christ, reconciling the world to himself, not charging them with their sins. And he has placed in us the Word of reconciliation" (2 Cor 5:18–19).

FOUNDATIONAL PRINCIPLES OF THE MUSHAKA RECONCILIATION PROCESS

On September 20, 2008, the leaders' meeting of the Ecclesiastic Basic Community (ECB) held that "every catholic church believer in MUSHAKA Parish convicted by Gacaca of killing people during the Genocide, or of participating in activities in which people were killed, must stop receiving communion and receive instruction during a six-month period, then show re-conversion."[2] [This divided] the actions of perpetrators into at least six categories of penitents determined by the Gacaca court. This sixth group is the focus of the first principles:

1. Catholic parishioners who committed acts of genocide must publicly ask for forgiveness in front of other parishioners.

In Rwandan culture, it was common that any person who had been found guilty of committing an atrocity was quarantined for a while to reflect, acknowledge, and repent of wrongdoing before being received back into the community, including its sacramental life. One who was baptized [but] then went on to break the commandments in such a serious way dishonors Christ present in the Holy Eucharist and cannot expect to receive Holy Communion in a worthy manner (1 Cor 11:27).

2. The criminal must personally ask for forgiveness from his or her victims.

Once they have asked forgiveness from the families of their surviving victims or family members, the perpetrator asks them to sign a paper acknowledging that this reconciliation has taken place. This is mandated by scripture:

> You have heard that it was said to the ancients: you shall not murder; whoever will have murdered shall be liable to judgment. But I say to you, that anyone who becomes angry with his brother shall be liable to judgment. But whoever will have called his brother, idiot, shall be liable to the council. Then, whoever will have called him, worthless, shall be liable to the fires of Hell. Therefore, if you offer your gift at the altar, and there you remember that your brother has something against you, leave your gift there, before the altar, and go first to be reconciled to your brother, and then you may approach and offer your gift. (Mt 5:21–24)

3. The genocide survivor is asked to forgive the one who inflicted harm.

Forgiveness is the medicine that cures the wounded soul. Those who committed acts of violence must reveal the truth about the fate of family members. And by offering such extraordinary, sacrificial forgiveness, survivors reveal the truth of St. Paul's words, who said, "Do not allow evil to prevail, but overcome evil with good" (Rom 12:21).

4. A six-month period of special instruction must be offered to genocide criminals and victims.

During this time of weekly catechesis on Saturday, penitents learn about the following:

- life is a gift from God
- the commandments of God and the Church's moral law
- sin and its consequences
- the evil of ethnic discrimination and genocide
- wounds
- reconversion and forgiveness
- receiving God's divine mercy and new life in the Church

5. The role of victims in the reconciliation process

Forgiveness is the real remedy to cure physical and spiritual wounds. Forgiveness is a long process but is both necessary and useful for those who really want to recover. Just as someone with a physical disease will ignore the bitterness of the medicine, those suffering spiritual wounds must swallow the "bitter medicine" of forgiveness in order to recover. This process of recovery is called "reconversion."

6. A group of facilitators implements the program.

A group of facilitators is chosen among mature Christians—priests, nuns, nurses, survivors, and Hutu rescuers. This last category is especially important, because it prevents unilateral ethnic shaming. These facilitators helped in counseling and visiting both victims and penitents in their homes during the reconciliation process.

7. The goal is to rebuild relationships among "wounded hearts." Whenever possible, perpetrators must undertake some action to help bring healing to the wounds of victims.

Not all victims are ready to forgive right away. The perpetrator must be willing to show mercy through word and action, so that the wounds may begin to heal.

8. Victims must hold responsible the perpetrator, and only the perpetrator, for the wrongdoing.

His wife and children cannot do the work for the perpetrator, though they may often assist in beginning the process of unity and reconciliation. However, it is the perpetrator who must undertake the process personally. As we read in the book of James, "Therefore, confess your sins to one another, and pray for one another, so that you may be saved. For the unremitting prayer of a just person prevails over many things" (Jas 5:16).

9. The role of rescuers is crucial.

By their testimonies, rescuers remind parishioners of what they should have done: saving lives instead of spilling the blood of innocent people. Their presence reassures the victims, to see that not all Hutu are bad; it also challenges the perpetrators to see their crimes for what they are.

10. Reconciliation brings healing to the whole Church as well as the whole community.

By testifying to the reconciliation that has taken place, and giving thanks for the new life that is possible, both victims and perpetrators help the Church members and community members return to their original mission of respecting and protecting life. It creates new harmony within the communities and encourages those who are still outside to stop resisting the process of reconciliation.

11. This process of reconciliation ensures peace for future generations.

As they witness the efforts of the adults to work toward reconciliation, children are taught the importance of unity and peace. They will witness and benefit from acts of mercy, so that they do not fear any ethnic groups in their communities.

This helps to ensure the lasting peace in our churches and communities, and in the whole nation, as its next generation of leaders grows up to take their place in the world.

For more details on the catechesis program, go to "The Mushaka Peace Program" on Fr. Ubald's website, https://frubald.com.

Notes

Prologue

1. The First Congo War (1996–1997) led to the exile of all Rwandan and Ugandan forces from Zaire, which in 1997 became known as the Democratic Republic of the Congo.

Introduction

1. "Batwa" is the plural of "Twa."

2. Minor seminary refers to the three years of secondary school, typically a boarding school, for those interested in becoming priests. This is followed by another four years of college-level seminary training at a major seminary.

3. Referenced in 1 Corinthians 12:8, the gift of knowledge is a spiritual gift or grace by which the Holy Spirit reveals to an individual something that could not be known on a purely human level, for the benefit of those present. As the *Catechism* tells us, "There are furthermore *special graces*, also called *charisms*, after the Greek term used by St. Paul and meaning 'favor,' 'gratuitous gift,' 'benefit' [cf. *Lumen Gentium* (*LG*; On the Church), 12]. Whatever their character—sometimes it is extraordinary, such as the gift of miracles or of tongues—charisms are oriented toward sanctifying grace and are intended for the common good of the Church. They are at the service of charity which builds up the Church" (cf. 1 Cor 12; *CCC*, 2003).

1. The Night of the Sword

1. "Mutwa" is another term for the Twa ethnic group.

2. Banana beer (*urwagwa*), a homemade brew made of pressed banana juice and sorghum flour, is in high demand in Rwanda, as it is three times cheaper than ordinary beer and three times as strong. See Jean Hatzfeld, *Machete Season: The*

Killers in Rwanda Speak (New York: Farrar, Straus, and Giroux, 2005), 6.

3. Among the Rwandan and particularly for the Tutsi, the number of cows a family owned directly reflected on their position in the community. During the genocide, the killers would often slaughter the livestock to further humiliate their victims before they died. After the killings, the perpetrators would sometimes have great barbecues to strengthen them for the next day's "harvest."

2. Blood on a Thousand Hills

1. In an interview on June 19, 2018, Fr. Ubald's brother Révérien, who was then personal assistant of the secretary general of the RPF, stated, "The RPF and the Rwandan government had been in peace talks, and so the plane crash was a surprise for us—we were expecting a peaceful end due to the political negotiations. Six hundred RPF soldiers were in Kigali, ready to integrate forces into a transitional government. When the plane crashed, the situation changed even in our own minds. What was more surprising, just minutes after the crash, the killings started throughout the country." Today Révérien is part of a Rwandan Formed Police Unit, providing special support services such as monitoring and escorting, to ensure the ongoing peace and safety of Rwanda.

2. The extremists also targeted Hutus who were in opposition to the government. The Hutu killed without mercy—even Tutsi babies, who might one day grow up to reclaim the land their parents had once occupied. In reality, there were no RPF living in Rwanda at that time. The RPF was composed of refugees who were fighting for the right to return to Rwanda; some had parents who had fled from Rwanda in the 1960s. But it didn't matter.

3. Hatzfeld, *Machete Season*, 106.

4. Members of this order later formed the Missionaries of Peace, an order of religious brothers and sisters founded by Sr. Donata Uwimanimpaye, who works with Fr. Ubald for reconciliation in Rwanda.

5. Cindy Wooden, "Pope Apologizes for Catholics' Participation in Rwanda Genocide," CNS News, March 29, 2017, http://www.catholicnews.com.

6. At the time, fifty thousand Rwandan francs was equal to about seventy US dollars.

3. *"Take Up Your Cross, Ubald"*

1. Timothy Longman, *Christianity and the Genocide in Rwanda* (London: Cambridge University Press, 2011), 186.

2. These five keys are based on the teaching of Neal Lozano in his book *Unbound: A Practical Guide to Deliverance* (Grand Rapids, MI: Chosen Books, 2003), 19.

3. The Emmanuel Community is a Catholic charismatic prayer association founded in 1976 by Pierre Goursat and Martine Lafitte-Catta. They are devoted to living in community a life of prayer, evangelization, and compassion for the spiritually and materially poor. For more information, go to http://emmanuelcommunity.com.

4. *Making Peace with the Past*

1. Longman, *Christianity and the Genocide in Rwanda*, 163.

2. Thaddé Ntihinyurwa, archbishop of Kigali, "Rwanda: A Dual Jubilee of Hope and Peace," April 1, 1998, http://www.vatican.va.

3. The word *gacaca* may be loosely translated as "justice seated on the soft grass."

4. See "Legacy Preservation," Gacaca Community Justice, accessed April 21, 2018, http://gacaca.rw.

5. The Missionaries of Peace, who are discussed in chapter 7, receive formation training in "Christian listening," a healing technique that originated through Acorn Ministries in England. For more information, go to http://www.acornchristian.org.

6. *Stories of Eucharistic Healing*

1. Congregation for the Doctrine of the Faith, "Instruction on Prayers for Healing: Introduction," September 14, 2000, http://www.vatican.va.

7. A Vision of the Future

1. One resource that Fr. Ubald recommends for those who need to understand the stages of forgiveness is a book by John Monbourquette called *How to Forgive: A Step-by-Step Guide* (Cincinnati: Franciscan Media, 2000).

2. "Jeannette Kagame Preaches Love at US Prayer Breakfast," Rwanda Podium, February 8, 2018, http://www.rwanda-podium.org.

3. The documentary is available for purchase through http://www.secretofpeace.com.

Appendix

1. MINALOC, "The Counting of the Genocide Victims," final report, November 2002, Kigali, Rwanda, p. 19.

2. Commission of Peace and Justice, "Ba intumwa y'Ubutabera n'Amahoro," in *Peace and Justice Commission Journal* (Kigali, Uganda: Assumption 2012), 21.

BIBLIOGRAPHY

Carr, Rosamund Halsey, with Ann Howard. *Land of a Thousand Hills: My Life in Rwanda*. New York: Plume/Penguin, 2000.

Gourevitch, Philip. *We Wish to Inform You That Tomorrow We Will Be Killed with Our Families: Stories from Rwanda*. New York: Picador, 1998.

Hatzfeld, Jean. *Life Laid Bare: The Survivors in Rwanda Speak*. New York: Farrar, Straus, and Giroux, 2000.

———. *Machete Season: The Killers in Rwanda Speak*. New York: Farrar, Straus, and Giroux, 2005.

Ilibagiza, Immaculée, with Steve Erwin. *Led by Faith: Rising from the Ashes of the Rwandan Genocide*. Carlsbad, CA: Hay House, 2008.

———. *Left to Tell: Discovering God amidst the Rwandan Holocaust*. Carlsbad, CA: Hay House, 2006.

———. *Our Lady of Kibeho: Mary Speaks to the World from the Heart of Africa*. Carlsbad, CA: Hay House, 2008.

Longman, Timothy. *Christianity and the Genocide in Rwanda*. London: Cambridge University Press, 2011.

Lozano, Neal. *Unbound: A Practical Guide to Deliverance*. Grand Rapids, MI: Chosen Books, 2003.

Rugirangoga, Ubald. *Forgiveness: The Secret of Peace* (documentary). To order this film, go to https://frubald.com.

Fr. Ubald Rugirangoga has been a Catholic priest in the Cyangugu diocese of southeastern Rwanda since 1984. During the 1994 genocide, he lost more than eighty members of his family—including his mother—and more than 45,000 parishioners. During a trip to Lourdes, France, Fr. Ubald heard Jesus tell him to carry his cross: the genocide. In that moment, Fr. Ubald felt a release from the burden of his sorrows and knew he was called to preach healing, forgiveness, and reconciliation.

Fr. Ubald continues to focus his ministry on healing and evangelization. He travels the world offering Masses with healing prayers, from which there are many documented cases of physical, spiritual, relational, and emotional healings.

www.frubald.com
www.secretofpeace.com
Facebook: ubald.rugirangoga
Instagram: @secretofpeace
Twitter: @FrUbald

Heidi Hess Saxton is an award-winning Catholic author and an acquisitions editor for Ave Maria Press.

Immaculée Ilibagiza is an international speaker, Rwandan genocide survivor, and author whose memoir *Left to Tell*, published in 2006, was a *New York Times* bestseller.